The Wilderness
UNDERGROUND

The Wilderness

Underground

Caves of the Ozark Plateau

Text by **H. Dwight Weaver**

Photo editors **James N. Huckins**
and Rickard L. Walk

University of Missouri Press
Columbia and London

Copyright © 1992 by
The Curators of the University of Missouri
University of Missouri Press, Columbia, Missouri 65201
Printed and bound in Singapore
5 4 3 2 1   96 95 94 93 92

Library of Congress Cataloging-in-Publication Data

Weaver, H. Dwight.
    The wilderness underground : caves of the Ozark plateau / text by H. Dwight Weaver ;
  photo editors, James N. Huckins and Rickard L. Walk.
      p.   cm.
    Includes bibliographical references and index.
    ISBN 0–8262–0811–8 (alk. paper)
    1. Caves—Ozark Mountains.   I. Title.
  GB605.092W42   1992
  551.4'47'097671—dc20   91–37235
                                                                        CIP

◉™ This paper meets the requirements of the
American National Standard for Permanence of Paper
for Printed Library Materials, Z39.48, 1984.

Designer: Rhonda Gibson
Typesetter: Connell-Zeko Type & Graphics
Printer and Binder: Toppan
Typeface: Palatino

First half-title photograph: The action of water on stone shaped this high cylindrical dome.
Roy Gold

Title page photograph: The Giant Flowstone in Blanchard Springs Cavern, Arkansas, is one of
the most impressive speleothems of its type in the Ozarks. (Note: The cavers shown as a scale on
the top of the flowstone used great care to keep their clothes and footwear free of dirt and mud. In
retrospect, the photographers feel the use of people for scale in situations like this is a mistake
because of the potential for damage to irreplaceable beauty.) James Glock

Dedication page photograph: Cavers explore an underground stream passage. Terry Pitchford

Second half-title photograph: Formed at seemingly regular intervals, a multichambered cave
passage entices the explorer. Terry Pitchford

*Dedicated to the wise use and conservation
of the wilderness beneath the Ozark Plateau*

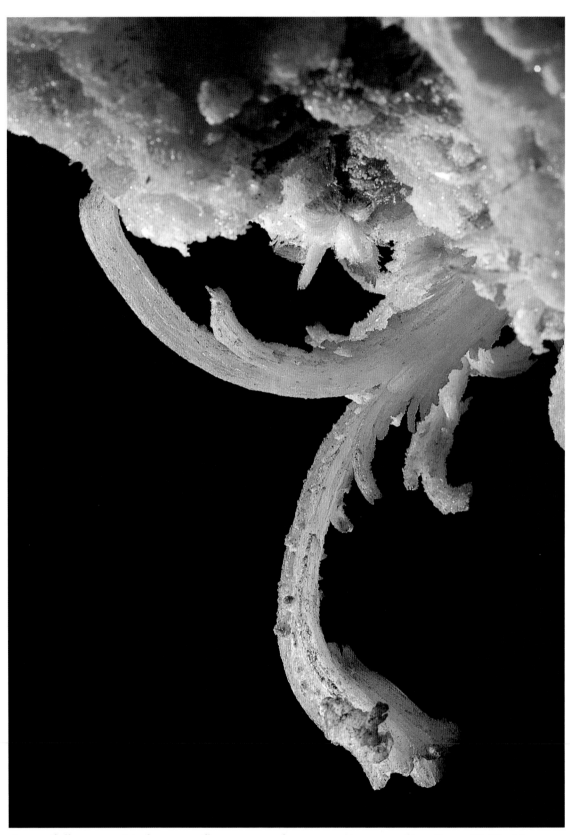

A gracefully symmetrical gypsum flower grows from a remote cave ceiling. James N. Huckins

Contents

A glassy calcite menagerie of helictites grows on a small ledge. James N. Huckins

Foreword

Jerry Vineyard

Ozarkians live in a region that is, in effect, a "cave factory" where caves form by natural chemical and physical processes. One may see caves in all stages of development, a rare privilege made all the more fascinating by the experience of going underground. Once formed, caves grow and change as geological processes shape walls, carve channels, and beautifully decorate the underground spaces with crystalline minerals. The same processes that form caves also destroy them when, in the eternal flow of geological time, the bedrock that the caves penetrate is removed by erosion and weathering, leaving behind remnants of cave structure that we call natural bridges, tunnels, and gulfs.

Geologists who study landscapes view the Ozarks as a region where the creative processes of cave-making are as active as at any time in earth's history—or perhaps even more so. The large springs in the Ozarks are caves aborning, where bedrock is dissolved and cave passages grow at phenomenal rates, geologically speaking. The saying "time is, man marches on" is especially apt because, compared with human lifetimes, the cycle of caves from youth through maturity to old age may seem very slow.

Of the many paradoxes linked with caves, none is more interesting than that of darkness versus light. Except for the feeble lights of explorers, and the rare bursts of intense light produced by photographers, caves are in eternal darkness. The pro-

cesses that shape caves and fill them with crystalline beauty operate in darkness that is absolute and never penetrated by the light of day. In the pages of this book, precious light is used in just the right way to bring out the incredible beauty hidden for eons beneath the familiar Ozark hills.

Equally important is the observation that people who venture regularly into caves usually develop a powerful conservation ethic. Why should this be? Caves are undeniably dark, damp, chilly, and usually muddy. Cavers returning to the surface after exploring caves are apt to be mud-covered from head to toe and chilled to the bone, but determined that the beauty and the fragile life-forms they have seen underground should be cared for and protected against vandalism and thoughtless pollution. Caving is generally enjoyed most by young people. As they grow older and their interests change, they become strong activists for conservation causes. Once "imprinted" by the caving experience, they rarely lose their conservation ethic.

The images in this book capture the essence of a remarkable era of discovery. Knowing that the Ozarks were first explored in the early 1700s, it is amazing to consider that over 90 percent of the known caves in the Ozark Plateau have been discovered and photographed in just the last thirty years. The existence of most of the large caves in both Arkansas and Missouri was not even suspected three decades ago. Not only have thousands of new caves been found, but advances in caving techniques and improved equipment have led to a better understanding of the caves through more complete exploration and scientific discovery. With the detailed cave maps now being produced, it is finally possible to consider realistically a cave's size and features, and not be misled by expansive and imaginative hearsay.

Individuals who have never experienced the exhilaration of discovering a new passage, a wonderful dripstone display, or the ten-thousand-year-old footprints of an ice-age lion in the damp mud of a cave floor may not appreciate the full meaning of some of these photographs, or the technical skills and physical exertion required to produce them. The photographs in this book represent the best in Ozark cave photography.

The author and master photographers whose work graces the pages of this book are cavers all. Reflected in the quality of the photographers' images is a genuine love for caves, and the hope that the features in the scenes captured on film will remain forever beautiful, conserved by the caver's credo: "Take nothing but pictures, leave nothing but footprints, kill nothing but time."

If this book tempts you to try cave exploration, remember that caves are places of potential danger as well as places of beauty. Never go caving alone. Always have three dependable sources of light for each member of the party, wear a hard hat, and tell someone where you are going and when you expect to return. Above all, join an organized caving club where you can learn about proper equipment and techniques and go caving with experienced companions. Finally, remember that the often innocent acts of touching cave mineral deposits and disturbing cave life can damage or destroy these wonders of the underground wilderness for generations to come.

This unusual gypsum flower is about two and a half inches in diameter and closely mimics the shape of a real flower. Dennis Taylor

Acknowledgments

The idea for this book began as a collaboration by Edward D. King, formerly director of the University of Missouri Press, and his colleagues, Susan McGregor Denny and Rick Boland. Their search for cavers willing to undertake the project led them to Chouteau Grotto, a Columbia caving club, and friends. Through many long months that followed, Susan Denny's nurturing saw the project take shape and the manuscript become a reality. Jane Lago guided the project through its final stages to fruition as a book. They have our heartfelt thanks for their patience, guidance, and inspiration.

The author is grateful to Jeannie Pridmore of the National Speleological Society, Emily Davis Mobley of Speleobooks, and to Bill Palmer, James Glock, James Huckins, Rickard Walk, Robert Taylor, Arthur Hebrank, and Michael McIntosh for encouragement and technical assistance.

To Jerry Vineyard, the author and photo editors give a hearty thanks for providing a superb foreword. Appreciation also goes out to Dennis Figg, Richard Clawson, Dr. Oscar Hawksley, Dr. Wilbur Enns, Eugene Vale, the Missouri Department of Natural Resources, the Missouri Department of Conservation, the Missouri Speleological Survey, the Arkansas Game and Fish Commission, the U.S. Forest Service, the National Park Service, and the National Speleological Society.

The manuscript made its greatest leap to a successful conclusion through the efforts of knowledgeable readers. To them we say thanks.

The photo editors also recognize the assistance and encouragement of the individuals who spent many hours in a dark room reviewing endless cave slides to make the selection used in the book. They include Susan Denny, Richard Boland, Dwight Weaver, James Glock, Robert Taylor, James Ruth, Kevin Feltz, and Chouteau Grotto friends.

Some of the photographs, particularly those taken in Blanchard Springs Cavern, represent the combined effort of several of the photographers who contributed to this book. Most of the cave photographs, with the exception of close-ups, would not have been possible without the tireless work of many unmentioned cavers who held flash units or posed in difficult positions and uncomfortable places.

For the support of many of the cavers of the Ozark Plateau, we say thanks.

The Wilderness
UNDERGROUND

Water seeping from the ceiling joint of this side passage has decorated it with translucent drapes.
James N. Huckins

Ozark Wilderness Underground

Since the middle decades of the twentieth century, thousands of caves have been discovered beneath the hills, ridges, valleys, towns, and cities of the Ozarks. More than 6,500 air-filled caves have been located in the 60,000 square miles of the region's rugged, hilly, forested terrain. Almost daily, newly located caves are named, recorded, and mapped by cave explorers. No one knows how many caves will eventually be found in the Ozarks. The present inventory is thought to represent only a modest percentage of the potential.

The caves of the Ozark Plateau, seemingly legion in number and primitive in their form, are varied in many ways. Though shrouded in darkness, silence, and solitude, they hide remarkable beauty. This beauty exists beneath the surface of an often exploited, ever more polluted Ozark landscape. But many of the caves that lie beneath the Ozark landscape still meet all the criteria that define a wilderness.

The concept of caves as underground wilderness is a new idea, even newer than the Wilderness Act signed into law by President Lyndon B. Johnson in 1964. That act created a wilderness protection system in the United States that preserves millions of acres of the nation's finest pristine beauty by keeping it safe from the impact of civilization. The act defines wilderness "as an area where the earth and its community of life are untrammeled by man, where man . . . is a visitor who does not remain."

Thus, wilderness is uninhabited land where human activities are essentially unnoticeable. All of the large caves known in the Ozarks have secrets. Most of the undiscovered and unexplored caves are as pristine as when nature created and refined them millions of years ago. Although graffiti and vandalism have marred the beauty and adversely affected life in many Ozark caves, especially those in densely populated areas and those easily reached by road or highway, numerous caves of the Ozark Plateau contain only footprints to bear witness to the passage of people.

Wilderness is land that bestows the feeling of being remote and beyond the influence of civilization. To step through the entrance of an Ozark cave and venture into its wet, rock-walled interior is like stepping into a different world. Go any distance at all and you leave behind most things familiar and comfortable. Even the sounds of civilization vanish as the solitude of the cave's environment surrounds you.

The need to protect the fragile quality of Ozark caves was recognized a century ago by Luella Owen, one of Missouri's pioneer speleologists. "The caves in this region have been deprived of great quantities of their beautiful adornment by visitors," she wrote. "The gift of beauty should always be honored and protected for the public good."

In 1975, the Missouri Department of Natural Resources, supported by the Missouri Department of Conservation, the Missouri Speleological Survey, the Mis-

Dissolved minerals impart a deep azure blue to the water of this rimstone pool. James N. Huckins

souri Caves Association, and others, began an organized effort to protect Missouri caves. Their work resulted in passage of the Cave Resources Act in 1980 by the Missouri legislature. This act recognizes the value of caves by establishing specific penalties for vandalism and providing cave owners with legal authority to protect their caves from trespassers. It also offers protection both to the rock surfaces of the caves and to the natural materials they contain, such as stalactites, stalagmites, cave life, and paleontological remains. Since its establishment, the Missouri Cave Resources Act has been used successfully to prosecute violators who have committed acts of vandalism and trespass.

In 1989, the Arkansas legislature enacted the Arkansas Cave Resources Protection Act to protect that state's portion of the Ozark underground wilderness. The Arkansas legislation gives special protection to endangered gray bats, the Ozark cave-fish, grotto salamanders, and several species of invertebrates. Similar measures may be taken in the near future by Oklahoma to protect its Ozark cave resources.

A delicate gypsum curl lies on a cave floor, perhaps broken by careless human contact. James N. Huckins

The Boston Mountain Range in northern Arkansas is one of the most rugged areas in the Ozark cave region. James Ruth

Ozark Cave Country

The cavernous Ozark region, which is the largest extensively elevated landmass in the United States between the southern Appalachians and the Rocky Mountains, is one of North America's finest cave regions. Geologists call it the Ozark Uplift; geographers, the Ozark Plateau. The plateau covers approximately 40,000 square miles of southern Missouri, 16,000 square miles of northern Arkansas, and 4,000 square miles of northeastern Oklahoma. The extreme southeast corner of Kansas contains fewer than 100 square miles of Ozark terrain. In its entirety, the plateau is roughly 300 miles long by 170 miles wide.

Age clings tenaciously to every bare rock of this land, which is known to have geological roots more than a billion years old. The cave region is noted for its ridges of fossiliferous, cherty limestones and its undulating hills of magnesium-rich dolomites. Its canyonlike valleys have been etched into the landscape by free-flowing streams, and its thin-soiled rocky slopes are covered with oak, pine, and hickory forests. The plateau has many cold freshwater springs with a total discharge of billions of gallons of water daily. Streambeds in the region often swallow their flow like thirsty sponges, and some of the region's plains and basins are cratered by tree-rimmed, brush-choked sinkholes and rock-walled pits. Where streams have entrenched the landscape, bluffs of layered rock are often left pockmarked by cavities and cave openings.

The rivers that generally separate the bluff-lined northern boundary of this uplifted region from surrounding lowlands include the Osage and the Missouri. The Mississippi River, to the east, separates the region from Illinois. The Black River parallels its southeastern edge, where the Mississippi River embayment opens to vast alluvial flatlands. The Arkansas River borders the region's southern extremities, and the Neosho River, the western edge.

All of the streams that spring from the

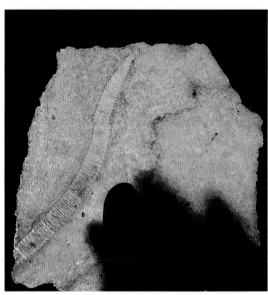

This gypsum crust fragment with a crinoid stem imprint was found on a well-used cave pathway. Because of its imminent destruction, the photographer carefully moved it to relative safety away from the trail. (Note: Avoid touching speleothems; human contact damages them by leaving residues of oil, skin, and soil.) James Glock

The sun rises over cave country in the Ozark National Scenic Riverways, Missouri. Robert Glock

Fall colors adorn a dolomite bluff with a cave along the Jacks Fork River. James N. Huckins

interior of the Ozarks flow outward in a meandering, radial pattern to become tributaries of the encircling rivers. Many of the inland streams are spring-fed and fast-flowing. The Current, Jacks Fork, and Eleven Point rivers in Missouri, and the Buffalo River in Arkansas, are federally protected waterways of exceptional beauty.

The stream-laced, erosion-scarred face of the Ozark Plateau is gently saddle-shaped because its northeast and southwest extremities are higher in elevation than its interior. Several geologic and geographic subprovinces distinguish the plateau.

Arkansas Ozarks

The Boston Mountains extend across northern Arkansas as a range of high, stony hills underlain by shales, sandstones, and limestones. A profusion of summits characterizes the range, and the loftiest mountain crests at 2,578 feet. It is in this wil-

Rushing waters cascade from a cave entrance in a limestone bluff. James Ruth

derness country that the highest Ozark waterfall makes its plunge and the Buffalo River has its origin. For 148 miles the Buffalo River slices through cave-riddled rock and skirts high bluffs, creating scenic vistas.

Nearly two thousand caves have been discovered in the Ozarks of northern Arkansas. Some are huge and extensive, and many are well decorated with speleothems. A generous selection of these caves have been commercially developed for public visitation, and most are privately owned. Bull Shoals Cavern, located north of Flippin, is the centerpiece of a restored Ozark mountain village of the 1890s. Dogpatch Caverns, south of Harrison, is a well-decorated cave close to Al Capp's Dogpatch USA. War Eagle Cave, located halfway between Eureka Springs and Rogers, has a large entrance and huge breakdown blocks. Cosmic Caverns, north of Berryville, features an underground lake. Civil War Cave, west of Bentonville, displays a natural staircase of rimstone dams. Diamond Caverns is west of Jasper and is noted for its length and its slender stalagmite columns. Onyx Cave, northeast of Eureka Springs, provided torchlight tours for visitors from the mineral spas of Eureka Springs in the 1890s and is still a popular attraction. Hurricane River Cave, south of Harrison, features a waterfall.

Here, too, is Blanchard Springs Cavern, which is located northwest of Mountain View. The beauty of this enormous cavern, which is often called the "Carlsbad Caverns of the Ozarks," went undiscovered until the 1960s. The cavern has been developed for public visitation by the U.S. Forest Service.

Oklahoma and Kansas Ozarks

Where the Ozarks extend from Arkansas into Oklahoma's Indian country, the landscape is dominated by the Cookson

A rare cave shield speleothem (common in some other cave regions), resembling an angel's wing, grows from a wall beside a large stalagmite in Blanchard Springs Cavern. James N. Huckins

Missouri Ozarks

The largest portion of the Ozarks is in southern Missouri, where more than 4,200 caves have been located and recorded since the 1950s. Geographers divide this part of the Ozarks into the Springfield Plateau, the St. Francois Mountains, and the Salem Plateau.

Springfield Plateau

The Springfield Plateau hugs the western border of the Ozark Uplift in southwestern Missouri. Portions of this plateau touch Kansas and extend southward into Oklahoma and Arkansas. Low relief typifies the upland portions of the plateau, where elevations are close to 1,700 feet. Along the area near the White River headwaters, streams have entrenched themselves, creating narrow ridges and deep valleys that expose Ordovician dolomites that were formed nearly 500 million years ago. Near the Missouri-Arkansas border are hilltops that are almost devoid of vegetation. They are known locally as balds or knobs.

Springfield, the largest city in the Ozarks (population 143,000), is situated near the northeast edge of the plateau in Greene County, Missouri. The city sits upon a terrain that is punctured by thousands of sinkholes, many of which drain into caves.

The Springfield Plateau has an interesting variety of privately owned show caves. Fantastic Caverns, north of Springfield, is so large that tours are made by vehicle. Crystal Cave, also north of Springfield, is noted for its helictite room and the symbols left on its walls by Indians. Crystal Caverns, at Cassville, displays anthodite crystals that have formed on the cave's fossiliferous rock walls and ceilings. Bluff Dwellers Cave, a charming maze-type cave south of Noel, is named after the primitive

Hills, which are made up of 300-million-year-old Mississippian and Pennsylvanian limestone. Water has moved through them, creating hundreds of caves, many of which have yet to be explored and mapped.

The Ozark Plateau extends for only a few miles into the extreme southeast tip of Kansas where the state joins Missouri and Oklahoma. The Mississippian limestones that are so cavernous in southwestern Missouri thin rapidly on the Kansas side and do not have sufficient thickness to support significant caves.

In the confines of a cave passage, small cascades such as this can sound thunderous to the explorer. Robert L. Taylor

aboriginal bluff dwellers. Truitt's Cave at Lanagan and Ozark Wonder Cave at Noel were originally developed by J. A. "Dad" Truitt, the innovative "caveman" of the Ozarks. Marvel Cave, beneath Silver Dollar City, is the deepest cave in the Ozarks and is entered through a mountaintop sinkhole that opens into a gigantic underground chamber. Talking Rocks Cavern at Branson features a sound and music show that presents the cave's beauty and story in a dramatic way.

And near Protem is a cave called Tumbling Creek Caverns. It is the home of the Ozark Underground Laboratory, where cave scientists and students are at work unraveling the secrets of cave geology and studying the life cycles of animals that live in caves.

St. Francois Mountains

The uplands and hills of the Springfield Plateau bear little resemblance to the rocky highlands that distinguish the St. Francois Mountains near the northeastern border of the Ozark Plateau. The highest summit in the St. Francois Mountains rises to 1,772 feet above sea level about eighty miles southwest of St. Louis. These mountains form a 700-square-mile islandlike complex of rhyolite and granite peaks that expose the oldest igneous rocks in south-central North America, dating from 1.1 to 1.5 billion years ago. Caves are rare in this region because sedimentary dolomites and limestones have been largely eroded away and exist only in the deep, sheltered basins between the old igneous-rock knobs.

Evening light filters through a stream-traversed natural bridge. James N. Huckins

Salem Plateau

The heartland of the Ozarks is the Salem Plateau that surrounds the St. Francois Mountains. It spreads westward to the Springfield Plateau, south into Arkansas, and north to the Missouri River. It is the most extensive subprovince of the Ozark Uplift. The underground wilderness of the Ozarks extends beneath many segments of the Salem Plateau in southern Missouri, and caves seem to be everywhere.

The uplands of the Salem Plateau, ranging between 1,000 and 1,400 feet above sea level, survive as a rolling surface of low relief. But where streams have carved their channels deeply into the region's thick 500-million-year-old Cambrian and Ordovician rocks, bluffs 300 feet high are found. Some

narrow stream valleys are ancient unroofed caves whose original subterranean features have been destroyed through exposure to weather and erosion. Caves opening along the valley walls are usually accesses to remaining passages from once larger cave systems.

Streams that flow only after heavy rains are common to the karst landscape of the Salem Plateau. The word *karst* is generally applied to regions characterized by an abundance of sinkholes, caves, springs, and streams that lose their water to fractured beds of rock. Underlying the porous, chert-paved streambeds of the region are networks of old cave passages that pirate water from the aboveground streams. Any surface stream that loses a significant amount of its water to subsurface stream

The unique Angel Shower in Ozark Caverns, Lake of the Ozarks State Park, always flows with water, even during periods of drought. Terry Pitchford

A passage in Fisher Cave, Meramec State Park, Missouri, is almost completely filled with speleothems. Rickard L. Walk

cave systems, are in state parks managed by the Missouri Department of Natural Resources.

The Salem Plateau has a variety of privately owned show caves. Bridal Cave, north of Camdenton, is noted for its beauty and underground weddings. Jacob's Cave, located south of Versailles, displays speleothems and the bones of ancient animals. Fantasy World Caverns, south of Eldon, features an underground lake. Onyx Mountain Caverns, west of Rolla, is a huge cave once quarried for its beautiful onyx deposits. Rebel Cave, near Patterson, is in a locale famed for its legendary Spanish silver mines and Civil War history. And Meramec Caverns, at Stanton, is a large multilevel cavern that has an underground ballroom so spacious it will accommodate thousands of people.

The Missouri Department of Natural Resources manages several show caves in state parks of the Salem Plateau. They include Fisher Cave in Meramec State Park; Ozark Caverns, noted for its water-showering stalactites, in Lake of the Ozarks State Park; and spectacular Onondaga Cave in Onondaga Cave State Park. Onondaga Cave has a commercial history that dates from the St. Louis World's Fair of 1904.

Three outstanding rivers are protected in the Salem Plateau region. The Current River, the first stream to be designated a national scenic riverway in the United States, flows through Shannon, Carter, and Ripley counties in Missouri. In this Ozark National Scenic Riverway parkland, the National Park Service manages Round Spring Caverns as an educational attraction near the banks of the Current River. The Current River and its protected tributary, the Jacks Fork, feature more giant springs than any other river system in the Ozarks. Big Spring, midway along the Current's course at Van Buren in Carter County, is the largest spring in the Ozarks.

Southwest of the Current River water-

piracy is called a "losing" or "sinking" stream. Such streams are scattered all across the Salem Plateau and are a part of the drainage system sustaining the area's vast groundwater reserves, which in turn feed the region's springs.

Karst development has bestowed upon the plateau a marvelous assortment of caves and natural rock bridges. There are sinkholes that form huge sunken valleys and dewy, rock-walled natural underpasses that transect dolomite ridges and hills like abandoned railroad tunnels. The Salem Plateau has the largest concentration of springs in the nation, and two of the most spectacular chasms in the Ozarks—the Hahatonka chasm in Camden County, Missouri, and the Grand Gulf chasm in Oregon County, Missouri. These natural karst wonders, which are partially collapsed

The Tobacco Barn room in Round Spring Caverns, along the Ozark National Scenic Riverways in Missouri, was named for its large brown-colored stalactites, resembling bunches of tobacco hanging in a barn. James N. Huckins

shed, flowing through Howell and Oregon counties in Missouri, is the third protected river, the Eleven Point. Along the Eleven Point is Greer Spring, one of the largest springs in the Missouri Ozarks and famous for its wilderness setting.

The chasms, pits, natural stone bridges, springs, disappearing streams, and caves that distinguish the Ozarks comprise a remarkable collection of natural features. Their presence has added a unique dimension to the region's culture as well as to its geology.

Underground Mystique

There is a special mystique to caves that attracts many people. For some, caves offer the pursuit of knowledge and the prospect of new discoveries. For others, they provide a form of recreation. Each Ozark cave opening is a frontier, a boundary between the known and the unknown. To explore beyond that opening is to wander through the unknown toward mysterious horizons that cannot be seen but can be imagined.

The darkness of a cave generates unreasonable fear in some people, and the cold, clammy underground atmosphere often causes human discomfort. Bats, the creatures of medieval superstition, also dwell in caves. Except for natural beauty, the average person may feel that caves contain very little of value. In reality, caves are natural laboratories. They teach us about the relationships of living things to the environment, genetic adaptation, the structure of the earth, the development of landforms, and the secrets of the groundwater that is so essential to life.

Native American Exploration

The caves of the Ozarks have had their doorways open to man for thousands of years. American Indians were the first to venture inside them. The underground wilderness of the Ozark Plateau probably began to feel the impact of human activity as early as 10,000 B.C. with the appearance of the Paleo-Indian cultures of the Ozarks. It may have been these big-game hunters who helped to hasten the extinction of the mastodons, mammoths, jaguars, lions, and other large animals whose bones and teeth are now found in Ozark caves.

The advent of the Dalton Period of Indian history around 8000 B.C. saw the first occupation of Ozark caves. During this time, the Indians moved into the entrance chambers of accommodating caves. The smoke of hearth fires, and the human presence, undoubtedly had adverse effects upon the ecosystems of the caves, because the entrance zones of caves are very important to the animals that use caves as habitat.

The Archaic Period spanned 6,000 years, ending about 1000 B.C. The population of Indian cultures in the Ozarks increased dramatically during this period. More and more cave entrances were occupied. The Indians often relied upon caves as a source of water, for protection from the elements and from insect pests, and for clay for pottery. Some prehistoric Indians ventured deep into the darkness of Ozark caves using bundles of burning reeds for light. They went in search of minerals with ceremonial and medicinal value, such as gypsum, epsomite, mirabilite, and saltpeter.

Fundamental shifts in hunting and gathering strategies, and changes in modes of living, led the Indians out of the caves into river valleys and onto the uplands of

Sand ripples in a cave streambed and the ghosted image of a caver elicit the feeling of mystery often associated with caves. James N. Huckins

the Ozark Plateau during the late Archaic and subsequent Woodland Period between 3000 B.C. and A.D. 900. The Indians still used caves as a source of minerals and occasionally as burial sites, but for the most part they lived outside.

European Settlement

By the time the French and Spanish arrived on American shores in the late 1500s, 1600s, and 1700s, the Indians were well established in the forested lands of the Ozark wilderness. The impact of French and Spanish activities upon the underground wilderness was limited to sporadic mining of saltpeter deposits in caves for the manufacture of gunpowder. When settlers arrived from Kentucky, Tennessee, and Ohio after the Louisiana Purchase in 1803, the amount of saltpeter mined from Ozark caves increased substantially. This mining remained a thriving backwoods industry until the 1840s, when riverboat commerce began importing a better grade of gunpowder from eastern sources.

The early settlers of the Ozark hill country used caves for cold storage and waterpower. Spring flows and cave streams were harnessed to furnish power for the operation of sawmills, gristmills, and woolen mills. These uses probably did not have adverse effects upon the underground wilderness.

Nineteenth- and Twentieth-Century Speleologists

The caves and karst features of the Ozarks began to attract serious scientific attention in the 1880s. But the scientists who paved the way at first were unconventional—noteworthy in the fact that they were women, not men.

One of these scientists was Luella Agnes Owen, a geologist from St. Joseph,

Missouri. She was determined to examine the caves of the Ozarks and learn their origin. When she put on her divided skirts and sallied forth into the Ozark wilderness on horseback in pursuit of caves to explore, people shook their heads and wondered about her sanity. But Owen's brave perseverance prevailed. In 1898 she published the results of her explorations in a book titled *Cave Regions of the Ozarks and Black Hills of South Dakota*, which became a classic.

Ruth Hoppin, a pioneering biologist of the same period, explored Ozark caves in the 1880s looking for new species of life. Her discovery of the Ozark blind salamander in the caves of the Salem Plateau brought excitement to the halls of the Smithsonian Institution in Washington, D.C. After she sent the institution's scientists specimens of the pale little creatures, one zoologist pronounced them to be the most important zoological discovery on the North American continent in that day and time.

By the advent of the twentieth century, Ozarkians were beginning to discover the splendor and beauty hidden in the depths of their mountainous hills. It was rightly recognized by some that people would pay to see cascades of stone that resembled frozen waterfalls, glittering stalactites that needled cave ceilings, and massive stalagmites of crystalline rock. All that was needed were roads to the caves, steps for entry, safe underground trails, and guides. The era of the show cave had arrived in the Ozarks. Show caves have been a thriving Ozark industry for a full century, enticing millions of people to take a look at the marvels beneath the Ozark hills.

This new interest in caves raised many unanswered questions about their origins and their picturesque features. In the late 1930s, Willard Farrar, a young geologist working for what was then named the Missouri Geological Survey (today it is the Division of Geology and Land Survey

The cathedral flowstone displays a sharp demarcation in mineral staining. James Glock

Long linear passages of walking height found in some larger Ozark caves are a delight for cave mappers. John A. Lloyd

within the Missouri Department of Natural Resources), began a manuscript on Ozark caves. But World War II interrupted his research and claimed his life. His unfinished manuscript subsequently became lost. Only his partial list of cave locations survived.

With Farrar's list of caves, the urging of Missouri State Geologist Edward L. Clark, and the goodwill of Missouri's showcave operators, Dr. J. Harlen Bretz, a geologist at the University of Chicago, began his study of Missouri Ozark caves in the late 1940s. His first article on the subject, "Vadose and Phreatic Features of Lime-stone Caverns," was published in the *Journal of Geology* in 1942 and drew international acclaim. In 1956, his *Caves of Missouri* was published in book format by the Missouri Geological Survey. Both works have become classics.

Bretz solved many puzzles but raised just as many questions about the origins of Ozark caves and their features. His research became the catalyst that established speleology in the Ozarks and led to the founding of the Missouri Speleological Survey, a nonprofit organization of volunteer and professional groups devoted to the mapping, study, conservation, and preservation of Ozark caves.

In 1956, fewer than 400 caves were recorded in the Missouri portion of the Ozarks. Bretz visited fewer than 200 caves during his study. A remarkable era has unfolded in Missouri and Arkansas since then. More than 4,200 caves have been located, named, and recorded in the Missouri Ozarks, along with nearly 2,000 in the Arkansas Ozarks. Approximately 2,000 Missouri caves and 250 Arkansas caves have been mapped, and the work continues at a rapid pace. Missouri has more than 50 caves with more than a mile each of mapped passage, and one cave with more than twenty-eight miles. Many of the caves in Arkansas rival Missouri caves both in volume and in extent.

The truly large caves in the Ozarks have all been discovered in the past thirty years. On the threshold of the twenty-first century, the extent and nature of the underground wilderness of the Ozarks have been partly revealed. Many other discoveries await the future.

Daylight can still be seen from the bottom of this convoluted entrance pit. James N. Huckins

Ozark Bedrock

When you explore the creekbeds, bluffs, and hillsides of the Ozarks, you find many different types of rock. An easy search will yield fossil-bearing limestones, crystalline dolomites, grainy sandstones, crumbly shales, banded chert (flint), soft coals, banded rhyolites, and granites. Continued searching will turn up quartz, pyrite (fool's gold), galena, gypsum, and a wide variety of other mineral substances. This diversity of rocks and minerals makes the Ozarks geologically interesting and colorful.

Geologists subdivide layers of rock into units called formations. A formation is a layer or series of layers of rocks that have much in common yet are different from other natural units of rock above or below them. The common rock formations of the Ozark Plateau include buff-colored limestones, grayish dolomites, reddish sandstones, and bluish gray shales. Sandstone is a granular rock that consists of quartz grains cemented together with calcium carbonate, silica, and iron oxides. Shales are essentially thin-layered, or laminated, clays. Limestone is primarily the mineral calcium carbonate. Dolomite, a close relative of limestone, is primarily the mineral calcium-magnesium carbonate.

The bedrock strata of the Ozarks are predominately thick formations of limestone and dolomite intermingled with thinner layers of sandstone. These formations are usually hundreds of feet thick and may be stacked one upon the other to a depth of a thousand feet or more. It is in limestone and dolomite that Ozark caves have been formed because these rocks slowly dissolve when in contact with weakly acidic groundwater.

The study of rock layers is called stratigraphy. Each layer is like a page in a book of the earth's history. Its location, size, structure, mineral content, and fossils all provide information about past environments. The rock formations that make up the cave-bearing bedrock of the Ozark Plateau are sedimentary in origin, formed from sediments originally deposited beneath water. The typical horizontal orientation of these sedimentary formations tells scientists that the rocks were laid down beneath shallow inland seas that covered the region hundreds of millions of years ago. Geologists have divided sedimentary rock into stratigraphic units that represent intervals of geologic time, called eras.

The igneous rocks of the St. Francois Mountains are volcanic in origin and were formed more than a billion years ago during the Pre-Cambrian Era. This era was followed by the Paleozoic, Mesozoic, and Cenozoic eras. These three eras are the ones important to the history of the cavernous limestone and dolomite formations of the Ozarks.

The creation of the cave-bearing rocks of the Ozark Plateau occurred primarily during the Paleozoic Era. During each of its seven periods, many geologic events built and shaped the thousands of feet of sedi-

Cylindrical-shaped crinoid stem segments such as these often constitute much of the mass of the cavernous Burlington limestone. Rickard L. Walk

mentary rocks that make up the body of the Ozarks. Life evolved in the oceans and spread to the land. Inland seas came and went many times. Movements deep in the earth gradually raised the Ozark Plateau, creating what geologists call the Ozark Uplift or Ozark Dome. Eventually, the region was elevated enough to prevent the return of the inland seas. Forests and vegetation then spread across the face of the land. In the millions of years since then, erosion has been at work to create the deep valleys, bluffs, ridges, hills, basins, and plains that define Ozark topography.

Water always seeks the lowest level. It labors to reduce any elevated landmass to base level by stripping away soil and rock. The uplift gave Ozark streams steeper gradients to do this work. Since the layered bedrock of the plateau varies in composition, structure, and thickness, the erratic forces of erosion have left the Ozark Plateau cluttered with partially eroded, isolated uplands, mountains, and natural rock features that survive like relics in an ancient landform museum.

Groundwater Secrets

Not all of the shaping of Ozark topography was a surface phenomenon. While surface streams did their work, groundwater was doing its share by dissolving rock beneath the plateau, leaving it perforated with sinkholes, pits, and caves.

Groundwater is any water that is found below the surface. When rains occur, some surface water is absorbed by vegetation, and some becomes runoff that forms streams and lakes. Most of the remainder infiltrates the porous structure of soil and rock and percolates downward. It also gains access to bedrock through joint systems. Sedimentary rock layers have many natural fractures called joints, which are caused by expansion and contraction of the earth's crust. The bedrock strata of the Ozarks are riddled with these generally vertical fractures, which together form intricate sets or systems of joints.

Modern highway engineers have sliced into Ozark hills, creating many road cuts that expose a variety of rocks. Examining road cuts is an easy way to study the uppermost layers of Ozark bedrock. The horizontal bands of exposed stone are stacked like the layers of a cake. The meeting of two rock layers is called a bedding plane. These horizontal structures also conduct groundwater. It is along the intermingled joint systems and bedding planes that groundwater descends and where many Ozark caves have developed.

The water entering bedrock strata passes downward through the zone of aeration where the partings and pore spaces of the rock are mostly air-filled. Eventually it reaches a zone of saturation where rock partings and pore spaces are water-filled. The upper surface of this zone, where the aerated rock and the water-saturated rock meet, is called the water table. The elevation or level in the bedrock at which the water table stands is established by the surface stream in that drainage basin with the lowest elevation. Underneath hills divided by stream valleys, the upper limit of this saturated zone is generally higher. Nonetheless, the water table is much closer to the surface beneath valley floors than it is beneath hilltops and uplands. A water well drilled on an upland may have to be sunk several hundred feet to reach the water table and the saturated zone below it.

Formations of rock that can store and supply usable amounts of groundwater to wells are called aquifers. Porous sandstone and fractured layers of limestone and dolomite allow groundwater to flow through them. However, the movement of groundwater is not uniform because conditions in aquifers vary from area to area. The level of the water table below the surface can fluctuate in times of heavy precipitation or drought. Water-pressure hydraulics can force water to move uphill or rise vertically, as exhibited by the surges with which water boils to the surface at the outlets of some Ozark springs. But under ordinary conditions, groundwater flows like water on the surface—downhill. If a valley intersects the

Known for its clarity and azure-blue color, Blue Spring in the Current River watershed of Missouri is particularly attractive during the early fall. James N. Huckins

water table, groundwater may escape to the surface as a spring.

Generally, water travels very slowly through an aquifer, moving only a few feet per year. But in the karst terrain of the Ozarks, it can flow more rapidly because of enlarged fractures and well-developed underground channels. It may take the water only a few hours or days to travel ten or twenty miles beneath the surface. It is the infiltration of rainwater that keeps aquifers charged with groundwater. The Ozark Plateau is super aquifer country, and the water-bearing layers of bedrock have been soaking up, storing, and transmitting groundwater for millions of years.

Groundwater passes fairly rapidly downward through the aerated zone on its way to the water table. Where the bedrock has partly open joints that reach the surface beneath the soil cover, these joints may act as funnels for water flow. This allows the groundwater to leach or wash away the soil covering the joint. The soil is carried down with the water, and a conical or bowl-shaped depression forms in the surface soil of the landscape. When this happens, a sinkhole is born. The larger a sinkhole becomes, the more water it collects. Occasionally groups of sinkholes coalesce and form a sinkhole valley. A sinkhole with an open pit or passage at its base may lead into a cave, but many sinkholes do not drain into a human-sized rock opening.

Excellent examples of this kind of topography can be seen at Ha Ha Tonka State Park in Camden County, Missouri. Here, one of Missouri's largest springs discharges at the head of a chasmlike valley. Giant sinkholes and sinkhole valleys, a natural bridge, and other karst features in close proximity to each other let the observant visitor see how these features are interrelated and how the karst landscape evolves in the Ozark Plateau.

Into the realm of darkness, cavers enter the sinkhole entrance of a large wild cave.
James N. Huckins

Cavers return from darkness into the world of light, leaving the same wild cave. John A. Lloyd

A large cave entrance discharging a small stream is typical of many Ozark caves.
Emmet R. Anderson

Cave Origins

Until recently, it was generally thought that most caves in limestone and dolomite bedrock were formed almost entirely in the aerated zone by the dissolving action of acidic groundwater as it seeps or flows through joints and bedding planes. But modern studies have shown that most cave development actually begins at the level of the water table, or just below it in the saturated zone. It is here that groundwater collects in volume in joints and bedding planes and has the greatest amount of time to do its work.

Groundwater can slowly dissolve limestone and dolomite because it is enriched with carbon dioxide. The chemistry actually begins before the water even reaches the cave-forming bedrock. Raindrops dissolve very small amounts of carbon dioxide from the atmosphere. When the water enters the soil, it absorbs a great deal more carbon dioxide from decomposing organic matter in the soil. The combination of CO_2 (carbon dioxide) and H_2O (water) produces H_2CO_3 (carbonic acid). This weak acid is capable of dissolving the minerals calcium carbonate and calcium-magnesium carbonate, the soluble cementing agents that hold the insoluble rock portions of limestone and dolomite together. Most caves in the Ozark Plateau probably owe their existence to the dissolving power of carbonic acid. But it is also possible that some cave development has been influenced by sulfuric acid, which may be produced from sulfur-containing minerals of lead, zinc, iron, and other elements present in many bedrock layers.

The latitude and relatively low elevation of the Ozark region provide for a fairly temperate climate. These factors, plus an average rainfall of forty inches per year, permit thick vegetation and contribute to high amounts of carbon dioxide in the soil humus. This maintains a high level of groundwater acidity during all but the coldest months of the year.

Groundwater is continually at work beneath the soil, which is very thin in the Ozarks, dissolving the carbonate bedrock. This form of weathering leaves behind insoluble residues composed of chert, quartz, sand, and other solids. Ozark creekbeds, hillsides, and hilltops are often covered with this gravelly debris. The streambeds inside Ozark caves are often paved with the same loose material.

In the water-saturated zone, the acidic water begins dissolving the rock. As the water-filled fracture grows larger, it collects more water and enlarges faster. Turbulence and water flow increase, altering patterns of solution. The water also carries particles of rock dislodged by the solution process. These may be swept along and act like sandpaper to abrade the rock walls of the channel.

The dissolving power of the acidic groundwater that circulates through the massive bedrock formations of the Ozarks is illustrated by what is occurring at Big Spring in Carter County, Missouri. Ground-

Big Spring in Carter County, Missouri, is the largest single spring outlet in the Ozarks, and it is forming a vast cave system. Robert Glock

water rises from this spring at the average rate of 276 million gallons daily. In times of peak flow, after sustained periods of precipitation upon the spring's watershed, the discharge may reach 800 million gallons per day, creating an impressive riverlike flow.

The water rushes upward under artesian pressure from the still unexplored water-filled depths of the hills near the spring. The artesian pressure is produced by the weight and volume of excess water stored in the aquifer that feeds the spring. The water bursts forth in a dramatic "boil" that carries with it tons of dissolved dolomite. On an average day the water removes 175 tons of carbonate rock from bedrock in Big Spring's underground watershed. This amounts to nearly 63,875 tons per year.

This solution process has been underway for thousands of years. A very large cave-spring system is collecting and gener-

ating the water flow, with most of the water coming from the spring's watershed to the south and west of the outlet. In fact, some of its water flow has been traced by scientists from the Ozark Underground Laboratory to sources forty miles away.

The water table, from which most large Ozark springs discharge, does not have a static level. Its vertical movement depends upon the amount of rainfall. Sustained periods of wet weather may raise it ten, twenty, perhaps even fifty feet or more. Once the rains cease and the recharge of the water table is lessened, it slowly declines until it is once again at its normal elevation. This fluctuation has a definite effect upon cave development, extending the cave-making range of the acidic water.

Ozark caves develop in a variety of patterns. A cave may become one long meandering linear tunnel with no side avenues, or it may have a major trunkline corridor with numerous small side passages

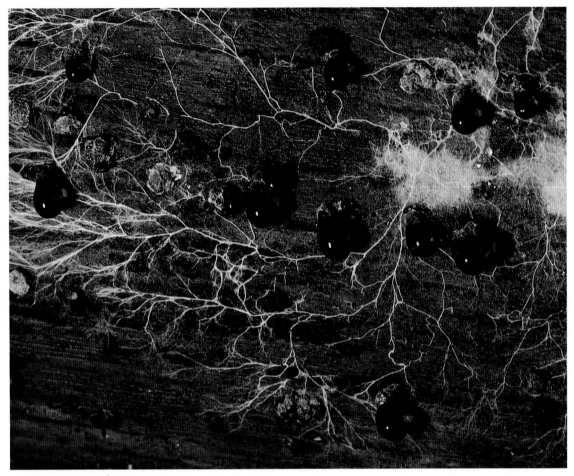

Unusual droplets of resin and fungus decorate a log that was washed into a cave by a losing stream. James N. Huckins

that give it a treelike design. Occasionally, caves assume mazelike patterns and become labyrinths of passageways on one level or several intermingled levels.

As surface valleys are deepened through the down-cutting action of streams, the water table gradually descends to lower elevations. The groundwater permanently abandons old conduits in pursuit of new ones, and former water-filled channels become permanently air-filled. But this does not always end the usefulness of the old channels. They may continue to serve as routes for groundwater flowing through the aerated zone to the water table. These streams can modify cave features through further solution or through abrasion by waterborne sediments. Such streams also may deposit sand, gravel, and clay. It is these abandoned passages in the aerated

zone that so often pirate surface water in karst terrain and create sinking surface streams.

The processes of erosion on the surface and solution underground operate continually, but it may take thousands or millions of years for them to create visible or dramatic changes in surface topography. When eroding surface streams in the process of deepening their valleys encounter old air-filled caves, the caves may lose their rock cover and be left exposed to become canyons or chasms like those seen at Ha Ha Tonka State Park and Grand Gulf State Park. When this happens, the process may also leave a segment of cave roof intact on the surface, creating a rock bridge. The chasms featured at these parks are karst in origin and display rock spans associated with giant sinkholes and collapsed cave

This dry cave entrance high in a bluff overlooks the pastoral beauty of river-bottom farmlands. Emmet R. Anderson

passageways.

Throughout the Ozark Plateau caves are found at various elevations. Sometimes cave entrances are high on the face of a bluff and inaccessible to everyone except cavers with climbing equipment. The existence of these high openings, and the ruggedness of the hills and valleys in the Ozarks, indicates that at one time long ago Ozark streams flowed at higher elevations. As they carved downward, dissecting the topography, they created bluffs and destroyed old cave systems, yet left behind many cave remnants. The creation of cave systems in the bedrock strata of the Ozark Plateau is currently occurring at the level of the giant springs that discharge from the bases of Ozark hills and in valley floors.

Today's air-filled caves are ancient by human standards but youthful on the scale of geologic time. Although a few solution features in some caves may be tens of millions of years old, most caves in the Ozarks have been formed more recently and have existed as air-filled cavities for fewer than ten million years.

Treasured Underground Beauty

The beauty of caves arises from a combination of qualities that give pleasure to the senses and exalt the mind and spirit. In the underground wilderness of the Ozark Plateau, beauty exists in mosaics of colors, textures, and shapes arranged in ways that create interesting spatial compositions. It is in the perfection of form attained by slow degree when groundwater chemically dissolves massive amounts of bedrock and creates new shapes that partially fill voids in limestone and dolomite bedrock. This kind of natural beauty excites human imagination and invites a person to step around the next corner to behold something new and different.

The most treasured qualities of underground beauty are those that delight the eye and appeal to the artistic senses. These qualities are embodied in water-sculpted

A large translucent gypsum growth is illuminated by strong backlighting. (Note: The hand visible behind this beautiful speleothem is holding the flash unit and is not in contact with the gypsum.) Dennis Taylor

This white crystalline flowstone in Blanchard Springs Cavern appears to be a relatively recent deposition. James N. Huckins

Clusters of exceptionally long, slender selenite needles transform a small ledge into a crystalline pincushion. Sadly, they were removed from this cave, a great loss to the underground wilderness of the Ozarks. Peter Chulick

rock forms called speleogens and in the varied deposits of loose or compacted layers of silt, sand, clay, gravel, and other sediments that carpet many cave floors. They also are embodied in the appeal of quiet lakes, trickling streams, thundering waterfalls, and in the crystal-faceted splendor of mineral deposits called speleothems.

Cave Diversity

Among geomorphologists and biologists, a cave may be defined as any natural opening large enough to transmit water, but for practical reasons explorers define a cave as any natural cavity in rock large enough for a person to enter and explore beyond the point of daylight. Horizontal cave openings in Ozark hillsides and bluffs range in size from openings so small they cannot be entered by humans to entrances large enough to accommodate a building eight stories high or half a city block long. The shape of the opening may be odd and unpretentious, or huge, scenic, and spectacular.

Caves that open vertically, as a pit in the ground, present a different kind of visual experience. To peer over the lip of a jagged pit that drops away into eternal darkness to some unfathomed depth can be unnerving to the uninitiated but exhilarating for the cave enthusiast. Most pits that open into Ozark caves are not large. They seldom exceed ten or fifteen feet in diameter, but there are exceptions. Few Ozark caves entered through a pit have a single vertical drop greater than a hundred feet, but here, too, there are exceptions. Frequently, pits bell out beneath the surface when they penetrate the ceiling of a spacious underground chamber.

Caves with pit entrances are of interest to scientists who study prehistoric life-

Warm sunlight and a mist-shrouded forest greet the eyes of visitors in the entrance passage of this cave. Kevin Feltz

forms because such openings have often been death traps for animals that once lived upon the Ozark Plateau. The conical debris piles of rock, soil, and decaying vegetation that rest at the bottom of most pits may yield the bones of extinct animal species.

Caves that must be entered through a pit present special problems to cavers. They also require specialized equipment that may include ropes, climbing hardware, and cable ladders. One should never trust old ropes, ladders, and other equipment left behind by previous explorers. Before entering a pit cave, it is essential to obtain the right kind of equipment and the assistance of experienced vertical cavers.

Many Ozark caves are small in height, width, and length. A large number extend only for several hundred feet, but at least 50 percent of the caves of the Ozark Plateau have several thousand feet of passage. Only about 3 percent of the recorded caves in the Ozarks are known to have more than

one mile of explorable passage, but this percentage may increase substantially as more exploration and mapping are undertaken.

Only one or two sharp bends in a cave passage are required to block the penetration of daylight. If a cold, spring-fed stream issues from a low cave opening, exploration can be a chilling and dangerous undertaking. Exploring a spring cave usually requires a wet suit. Some Ozark cave entrances are dry, but often springs are found flowing from caves. Since these streams generally react to heavy precipitation in a cave's watershed, experienced cave explorers exercise caution and do not venture underground when flooding is a possibility.

Interior Architecture

Internally, Ozark caves exhibit remarkable complexity. They vary from a single

This cave entrance shaft, one of the deepest in the Ozarks, is over one hundred feet deep and can only be entered by rope. Rickard L. Walk

This giant passage in Blanchard Springs Cavern is testimony to the slow but great dissolving power of groundwater. James Glock

A tunnel cave offers the path of least resistance to a small stream in Lost Valley, Arkansas. (The point of light is the opposite entrance.) Robert Glock

room or passage to a multitude of chambers of different sizes and shapes linked by passages that also vary in width, height, and configuration. Underground chambers more than 200 feet wide, 100 feet high, and 2,000 feet in length have been discovered in Ozark caves.

Caves may be composed of intermingled rooms and corridors on more than one level. In well-developed karst areas where pits and sinkholes are abundant, a cave may have more than one entry to the outside world. Caves that extend through a hill from one valley to another are called natural tunnels or tunnel caves. Associated with explorable caves are many erosional and solutional features that are collectively called speleogens. The arrangement, complexity, and refinement of these natural water-sculpted features is the essence of their charm. Although most Ozark caves are formed in horizontal layers

of bedrock that are basically flat in orientation, flat surfaces and smooth planes do not typify cave architecture. The arch, in one form or another, is the superstructure of most underground architecture because of its natural integrity and mechanical strength.

Nothing so dramatically reveals the architectural structure of a cave as passage cross sections. Cave mappers periodically draw these cross sections on their survey charts to depict structural features that cannot otherwise be easily shown on a two-dimensional map of the cave's floor. Cross sections are slices of a cave passage that depict the cave's outline at right angles to the linear direction of the cave passage. A thin slice of bread, for instance, is a cross section of the loaf. These passage cross sections help researchers visualize a cave's shape and volume. While passage shapes can be broadly categorized as round, oval,

Like light shining through the stained glass of a cathedral window, this beautiful arched entrance and its reflection are illustrative of the aesthetics of the entrance zone. Kevin Feltz

A keyhole-shaped silhouette or cross section of the main passage in Round Spring Caverns is revealed by partial lighting. James N. Huckins

Descending sheets of water formed vertical fluting in the limestone bedrock of this large dome.
Terry Pitchford

rectangular, triangular, or trapezoidal, the irregular surface of many cave walls, floors, and ceilings can make precise classification difficult.

No architectural form in the underground wilderness is as impressive as a deep pit in a cave floor or the towering spectacle of a dome in a cave ceiling. Whether a vertical shaft in a cave is called a dome or a pit depends upon how man views it. From the top, it is a pit. Seen from the bottom, it becomes a dome. If it is entered at any point between top and bottom, it becomes a dome pit. To climb a high dome or descend into a deep pit can be a hazardous undertaking, one that should not be attempted without the proper equipment and experienced companions.

Vertical shafts are usually the youngest major solutional features in caves. They develop along joints and fractures that may pass through any number of horizontal bedding planes. Rapidly descending groundwater cores the vertical shafts downward through the bedrock. They usually have a cylindrical shape and often have walls that exhibit vertical grooves.

Vertical grooves in cave walls or shafts are generally formed by whirls or eddies in thin films of acidic water, caused when the water flows over the uneven rock surface. Sometimes the grooves become curved and may extend from floor to ceiling. These speleogens can give cave walls a ribbed appearance.

Horizontal grooves are also created by water flowing through the cave. In an air-filled cave the upper surface of the water is sometimes held at different levels for varying intervals of time. This may be due to changes in the volume of water or to layers of sediment on the cave floor that elevate the streambed. The longer the stream can work at one level, the more it can incise a wall, eating away at soluble zones of rock and leaving resistant ones. This action produces horizontal wall grooves. As the soluble rock recedes, the grooves become

ledges and balconies of rock.

Enlarged joints are common Ozark cave features. They usually form at right angles to cave passages. When they are large enough to explore, they may lead to other passages. Frequently, enlarged joints are too narrow to enter and can only be examined by looking in with the aid of a light. The widening of joints also occurs in the early stages of cave development when the cave is forming below the water table.

When a cave stream is confined to a narrow meandering channel that switches back and forth from side to side along the cave floor, a meander-niche may develop where the curve of the streambed contacts the cave wall. In general, such a niche is an incised meander bend in the wall shaped like a crude arc or triangle. The cutting stream usually leaves a freestanding half-cone or triangular mass of bedrock in the center of the incised meander bend. This half-cone of rock was formerly a part of the wall and is now separated by the meander niche opening. Meander niches may become large enough to explore and walk through, but most niches seen in Ozark cave walls are very constricted, even though they may extend ten feet or more back into the wall rock.

If a cave stream is narrowly constricted along its bedrock floor for a long period of time, perhaps thousands of years, the water can carve out floor channels that often become canyons. Floor channels are fairly common in Ozark caves.

Channels incised upward into cave ceilings are less common. The development of ceiling channels is linked to fills that form when cave streams deposit sediments. If the cave passage becomes filled with clay, silt, sand, and gravel, the flowing stream finds itself pinned against the ceiling rock. Every new flood of water that comes rushing through brings additional sediment particles, which when carried in suspension abrade and wear away at the rock overhead like sandpaper. Eventually,

A balcony-like ledge in Blanchard Springs Cavern affords easy passage through an attractive room. James Glock

A profusion of densely packed soda-straws formed on a cave ceiling in an area with a multitude of joints and cracks. James N. Huckins

The rugged erosional features of this floor channel were created by an active cave stream. Rickard L. Walk

a ceiling channel is formed and becomes exposed when the hydrologic conditions of later streams change and erosion removes the sediments from the cave passage.

Cave streams that are confined against a cave ceiling sometimes go about their work of sculpting in a more complex fashion and produce pendants. Pendants are bedrock remnants that hang from a cave ceiling, or the underside of a ledge, like grotesque pieces of inverted sculpture.

Fast-moving cave streams frequently scallop walls. Scallops are shallow pockets or bowls. They are generally found on walls close to the cave floor where they mark previous high-water levels. The shape of a scallop can reveal the direction and speed of the water flow, since it will often have a steep slope on its upstream side and a gentler one on the downstream side.

When water totally fills a cave passage during the early stages of development, solutional activity can occur three-dimensionally. This may produce an interesting feature called spongework. Walls, floors, and ceilings become honeycombed with interconnected cavities. Spongework is a striking architectural form found in many Ozark caves. It gives the rock a wormholed, moth-eaten appearance. Complexes of spongework large enough to explore are not uncommon. After a cave becomes air-filled and a wet-weather stream invades it, spongework complexes may be altered by new solutional attack. An eroding cave stream may cut its way through the honeycombed stone, separating it into isolated displays of cavity-riddled rock.

Limestone and dolomite frequently contain other minerals. Chert, a hard, brittle stone often called flint, is commonly seen in walls, floors, and ceilings of Ozark caves. This insoluble rock becomes exposed as a cave is being formed below the water table or modified by later streams. The chert can be found as gravel or single chunks in streambeds and on cave floors. It may be smooth and water-worn or rough and sharp-

edged. Chert comes in a variety of agate-like colors that include mixtures of white, pink, brown, and black. These color variations are often hidden by dark manganese dioxide stains on the rock's surface.

Lenses, or layers, of thick nodules of chert are often seen protruding from cave walls, ceilings, and floors. These are rock inclusions not yet freed from the surrounding limestone or dolomite by the solution process. Such inclusions can produce natural bridges, ledges, and other interesting irregularities in caves.

The solution process in a cave does not always proceed smoothly. Chunks or blocks of stone are frequently dislodged or collapse from the ceiling and walls during the long course of a cave's development. This process is called breakdown, and the

The white limestone walls of this passage were carved and scalloped by a cave stream. James N. Huckins

These chert fragments, stained with manganese oxide, are a common feature of streambeds in Ozark caves. Emmet R. Anderson

Massive breakdown blocks constitute much of the floor of this dry, upper-level passage. Robert L. Taylor

An upper-level passage in Blanchard Springs Cavern is strewn with breakdown and a fallen giant column. James N. Huckins

blocks or fragments of rock produced by the process are also called breakdown.

Breakdown rock settles to the floor of a water-filled passage in the cave-forming stage. If these derelicts are not completely dissolved, they survive to become isolated boulders or great piles of breakdown on the floor of the cave. Even after a cave becomes air-filled, breakdown continues as the cave stabilizes and adjusts to the loss of its buoyant water.

Breakdown rock is a common Ozark cave feature and may be of almost any size from a small flake to a boulder as large as a house. If breakdown fills a cave passage, complete exploration of the cave may not be possible. Cavers should be cautious when climbing over, around, and through breakdown because the pile of rock may be unstable or have loose boulders that could easily shift and pin or crush an explorer.

Sediments

The sculpting of a cave provides a structure containing mixed voids in which nature continues to experiment, using water as the basic tool. Sediment deposition often follows water sculpting, or both solution and sedimentation may occur in the cave at the same time. Sediments are normally a mixture of compacted or loose materials such as clay, sand, gravel, silt, and organic debris from the surface. In addition to assisting in the creation of caves, these sediments also add to their beauty.

Ozark caves are infamous for red clay deposits. Sticky and tenacious, the clay adheres to almost any surface and is the bane of cavers. The red clay of Ozark caves is fine-textured and heavily pigmented with iron oxides that will stain clothing. It

Small deposits of red clay high in the complexly eroded main passage of Round Spring Caverns may be left from an earlier time when clay nearly filled many Ozark caves. James N. Huckins

served the former Indian inhabitants of the Ozarks as a source of pigment for their paints and clay for their pottery. Many Ozark caves were once filled or nearly filled with this red clay, but streams later invaded the caves, removing most of it. The scouring was not completed in every cave. The clay is often seen filling wall cavities and is found on ledges and floors.

Other gritty clay and mud deposits of rich chocolaty colors abound in Ozark caves. The sources of these sediments are the insoluble residues in the cavernous limestone and dolomite and materials imported from the surface by streams that have been pirated underground through sinkholes and cave entrances. The imported material is either dragged along the bottom of the stream course by the water or, if finer grained, carried down in suspension.

Because cave sediments can be millions of years old, scientists can tell a great deal about past environments that have existed in each cave's vicinity. Much of the imported material consists of organic debris or disintegrated rock particles derived from the weathering of surface landscapes. Even the flow velocities and discharge rates of ancient cave streams are revealed by the stratigraphy and nature of sediments that have been deposited.

Wet-weather cave streams are fickle. They may deposit sediments during one flood period and remove them during the next. Water-carved sediments often give stream banks fascinating profiles. More than anything else, sedimentation gives a cave its texture.

The Wonders of Water

Water, the sculptor of Ozark caves, is by itself a source of beauty. It saturates the cave atmosphere and impregnates the cave rock. It clings to all exposed surfaces, creates glassy pools and lakes, and forms streams that meander through the caves.

Atmospheric humidity levels fluctuate in the entrance zones of Ozark caves where outside and inside air are mixing, but in the more remote interiors of the caves, where total darkness reigns, humidity levels reach 100 percent. Cave air is, to some extent, always in motion, even though it may not be noticed. Cave features affecting air flow include the number of cave entrances, differences in distance and elevation between entrances, and the internal volume and structure of the cave.

Temperature differences outside between night and day, and between summer and winter, affect cave air flow. Changes in barometric pressure due to these temperature fluctuations or the passage of a weather front also create air flow and cause a cave to exhale or inhale like a living creature. If a cave opening exhales air during the cold of winter because of atmospheric changes outside, or because one cave opening is higher in elevation than another, water in the relatively warm cave air will condense on cooler outside surfaces such as vegetation near the cave opening. This can cause frost to form and surround the entrance with a winter scene of dazzling white beauty. Translucent ice stalactites and stalagmites frequently form in cave entrances during the winter. The statuesque shapes of ice formations are quite distinctive. If a cave with a stream is inhaling frigid air, the stream may freeze over for 100 feet or more into the cave's twilight zone or beyond.

Tiny pearly water drops will also condense on the fur of hibernating bats, on insects, on fungus gnat webs and spiderwebs, and on lichen growths within the cave's entrance zone. When hot summer days arrive, a change in barometric pressure may result in outside air flowing into a cave, causing fog or mist to develop in the zone of twilight between the entrance and the region of total darkness. Under certain conditions, mist and fog will even develop in the deep interior of a cave. Damp ex-

Frost covers a tree near the small entrance of a large cave. This type of frost forms when moisture-laden warm air from the cave freezes on cold surfaces outside the entrance. Rickard L. Walk

On exceptionally cold winter days preceded by wet weather, candlestick-shaped ice stalagmites form in some cave entrances. Daniel Drees

plorers can also generate vapor through their body heat and the process of breathing.

Underground streams, like surface streams, often meander. They dig out gullies in clay sediments and leave conical domes and buttes of clay between their loops. As a stream pursues its course it often disappears into wall niches and low openings. The stream may reappear further ahead in the cave passage or may disappear entirely. Sometimes a stream will disappear in one cave and reappear in another one nearby. Tracing these elusive paths can be educational as well as difficult. For hydrologists, knowing where a stream begins and ends is important in determining groundwater flow patterns and sources of potential pollution.

Underground streams in Ozark caves are seldom large enough to be classified as rivers. Only in times of flood do they carry huge volumes of water. But streams deep enough for boating do exist in some caves. Subterranean boat trips are sometimes necessary to gain access to a cave, but such trips are almost always fraught with stretches of low ceiling and shallow water or with difficult portages.

Lakes and streams in caves can also present other hazards for the cave explorer. Accidental drowning is an ever-present danger, even in underground streams and lakes not in flood. Overexposure to the

Tiny beads of water cling to the fragile web of a fungus gnat larva. James N. Huckins

Light from the photographer's flash reflects off a cave wall, creating a mirror image in a placid pool. Art Hebrank

coldness of cave water can cause hypothermia, which can be a subtle and deadly killer. Wet suits are essential for exploring a cave where extended immersion in a stream or a lake is necessary. If the water is deep and boats are required, they should have good flotation. Life jackets should be worn, and waterproof lights are needed. Experienced companions are a must.

Waterfalls are spellbinding additions to the underground wilderness, and show caves that contain them are envied attractions. Trickling or thunderous, waterfalls are inevitably entertaining. They are most likely to develop in Ozark caves after heavy rainfall and can be a source of alarm or concern to explorers. Waterfalls can also be a barrier to cave exploration. Even a waterfall that drops only a few feet can create a lot of sound in a cave. The noise is invariably amplified by its surroundings and may carry through the cave for a great distance as a muted, thunderous roar. It may seem to the explorer as if the very walls of the cave are throbbing with the rumble of the pounding water.

Water is the lifeblood of the underground wilderness of the Ozark Plateau—a kind of liquid enchantment that adds beauty, sound, and liveliness to a world where silence and solitude are the norm.

Speleothems

Speleothems are the most beautiful forms in the caves of the Ozark Plateau. They are the buried treasure of the show-cave industry, the trademarks by which much of the visiting public judges the quality of the underground attractions they tour. A cave devoid of speleothems seems somehow unfinished, unadorned, and uninviting to many people. Often inappropriately called cave "formations" (the term *formation* refers to bedrock strata), speleothems are mineral deposits that form by precipitation from mineral-rich water. Speleothem structures are wonderfully varied, encompassing the icicle shape of stalactites, the cylindrical rise of stalagmites, the towering majesty of columns, cascades of flowstone, folds of stone drapery, rootlike helictites, and a host of other distinctive forms.

Speleothems are fragile, natural creations of unique beauty that can be quickly and easily destroyed through human contact. Show-cave operators the world over carefully protect the integrity of the beautiful speleothems they display. Cavers often keep secret the locations of caves they find exquisitely adorned with speleothems. It is usually the desire to see such beauty that draws people to show caves. It is the desire to find and treasure such beauty that motivates many cave explorers.

In general, the traits that distinguish speleothems are form, fragility, and beauty. Though made of crystalline deposits, speleothems are just as fragile and subject to damage and destruction as are the exotic life-forms that live in caves. Exposed to the outside world, speleothems would quickly lose their beauty through deterioration brought about by weathering processes. Even when simply touched by visitors to the underground wilderness, they become discolored with the oil of human skin, smeared with sediments, broken, and destroyed.

A small ribbonlike waterfall plunges from the ceiling of a grotto. Robert L. Taylor

Heavy rains transform slow water seepage over these speleothems into a shower.
James N. Huckins

An unusual calcite speleothem represents the fusion of soda-straw and helictite forms.
James N. Huckins

Complex aggregates of calcite crystals are richly stained with the reddish-brown tint of iron oxide. James N. Huckins

A reflection in the pool at the base of the Giant Flowstone in Blanchard Springs Cavern conveys the perception of great depth. (Note: The cavers shown as a scale on the top of the flowstone used great care to keep their clothes and footwear free of dirt and mud. In retrospect, the photographers feel the use of people for scale in situations like this is a mistake because of the potential for damage to irreplaceable beauty.) James N. Huckins

In most cases, the minerals that form speleothems in Ozark caves have been leached by weak acidic water from adjacent rock. The water moves downward through vegetation and soil at the surface and collects carbon dioxide from decaying organic matter. Water and carbon dioxide blend to form carbonic acid. After entering the bedrock, the carbonic acid dissolves some of the limestone or dolomite, acquiring the minerals needed to build most speleothems. In caves of the Ozarks, these minerals include carbonates such as calcite and aragonite, nitrates often derived from organic sources, sulfates such as gypsum, and metal oxides.

Upon entering the cave, the mineral-laden water encounters the air in the cave, which has a lower carbon dioxide content than the air near the surface of the ground. This difference in the carbon dioxide content causes the carbon dioxide in the water to be driven out into the cave's atmosphere. This loss of carbon dioxide brings about precipitation of the minerals that had been dissolved in the water. A similar process (without mineral deposition) occurs in carbonated beverages that bubble or effervesce when exposed to air. The fizzing is excess carbon dioxide escaping.

In Ozark caves the environment is usually too humid to allow significant evaporation, yet the process of mineral deposition is sometimes misrepresented as a process of evaporation. In evaporation, the water passes off as a vapor; the liquid itself dissipates. But in the process of cave mineral deposition, very little of the water vaporizes—it only loses excess carbon dioxide and a small portion of its mineral content. Although less concentrated in dissolved substance, it still retains its visible liquid form.

Groundwater has decorated the caves of the Ozark Plateau with an amazing volume and variety of speleothems. The groundwater responsible for these lovely decorations often moves slowly. It seeps, drips, splashes, or moves in gentle flow while surrounded by air. Speleothems are formed drop by drop, but it may take hundreds or thousands of drops of water from the same rock fracture or rock pore to create a mineral deposit visible to the naked eye.

The growth rate of speleothems varies widely, even within the same cave. So many variables are involved that each speleothem has its own individual pattern of growth, the speed of which will change from season to season and year to year. Anything that affects the mineral content of the water, the acidity of the water, the volume of the water being supplied, or the place where the mineral is being deposited can affect speleothem growth. Thus, the growth rate of a cubic inch of speleothem can be anywhere from thirty years to thousands of years. Suffice it to say that, by human standards, the rate of speleothem growth in a cave makes a snail's pace seem supersonic. This is why speleothems should never be touched or broken. They are nonrenewable and irreplaceable.

Mineral growth is often interrupted by seasonal variations. If the water reaching a speleothem is less than fully saturated with mineral, for instance, re-solution is apt to occur. This can cause internal and external deterioration of the speleothem, resulting in cavities. Very small tubular speleothems are most vulnerable to this kind of structural damage. If the water supply stops for an extended period of time, the speleothem may become powdery and crumbly, even in the humid environment of the cave.

Speleothem shape is controlled by the crystal habit of the mineral and the manner in which the depositing water moves. Sheets of flowing water will typically leave thin, flat layers of mineral, while dripping water will concentrate the mineral into columnar structures. When calcite crystals are allowed to grow freely, without the influence of flowing water, long pointed crystals called dogtooth spar may develop.

Calcite crystal facets sparkle with reflected light on this dry cave wall. Slower growth rates generally produce crystals with large facets. James N. Huckins

A geode-like cavity in Blanchard Springs Cavern is encrusted with dogtooth spar crystals. James Glock

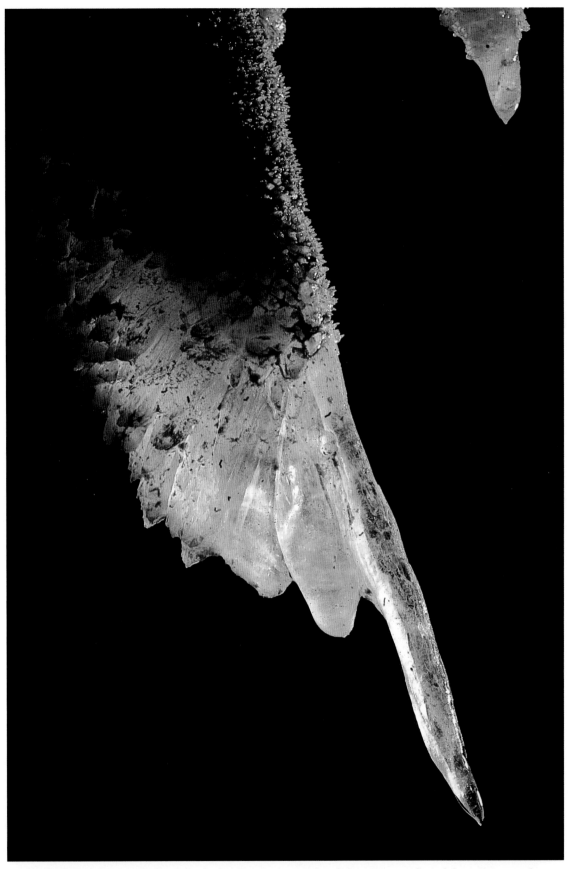

An eroded crystal-covered calcite "wing" is an example of changing cycles of deposition and dissolution. James N. Huckins

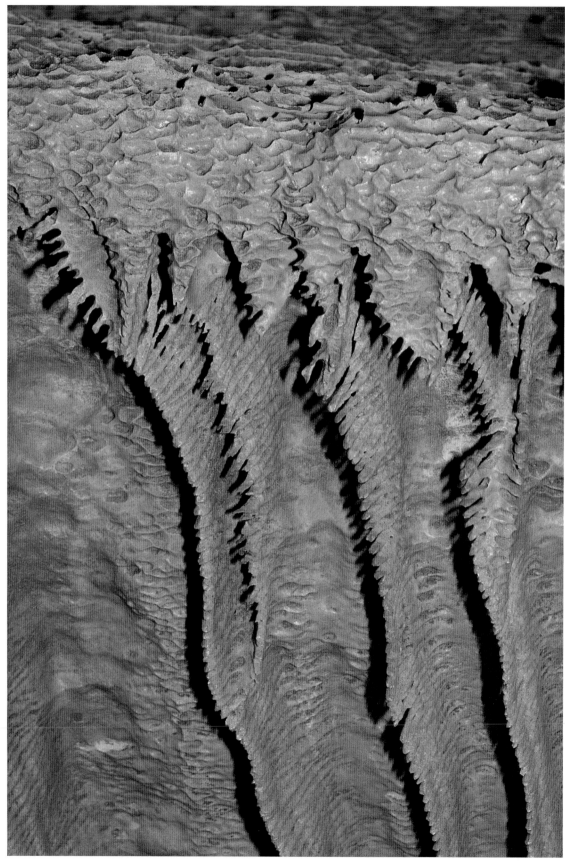

Feathered and pitted erosional features add beauty and dimension to the secondary mineral deposits on this cave wall. Rickard L. Walk

But within any class of speleothems many variations from the norm are possible due to the wide range of factors that influence their growth.

Speleothem color is the result of stains caused by impurities deposited between crystal grains. Mud and clay are a major source of speleothem color. Iron oxides will provide red and orange. Manganese oxides bring black, shades of charcoal, bluish gray, and pastel blue. Copper will produce blue-green. The purest crystals of calcite, aragonite, and gypsum are colorless and transparent, but trapped air in voids among the crystal structures usually creates whiteness.

Speleothems are not found in every Ozark cave, but most caves have at least a few. Ordinarily, speleothems are scattered along specific underground corridors or crowded into chambers separated by more barren passageways. Because joints in cave ceilings transmit water, quite often stalactites can be seen growing in straight lines along the course of a ceiling joint. Stalactites hanging from cave ceilings, stalagmites developing on cave floors, columns joining floor and ceiling together, and cascades of flowstone are the most common speleothem types found in caves of the Ozark Plateau, but there are many others as well.

When water drops precipitate calcite on a cave ceiling through the loss of carbon dioxide, the precipitation occurs around the outside of the water drop. The deposit is left as a ring, owing its initial shape to the circular shape of the water drop. Successive ring deposits begin the development of a narrow tube with thin walls and a hollow center that continues to convey mineral-laden water to its tip. In this way a soda-straw is born.

Soda-straws bring delicate beauty to caves. These fragile structures can transform a drab cave ceiling into a colorful, inverted pincushion of needlelike projections. The soda-straw is appropriately named because of its tubular shape and small diameter. Soda-straws occur individually and in dense clusters. Left undisturbed, they may grow to lengths of six feet or more, but they are typically less than two feet long in Ozark caves.

Variations occur in the soda-straw family, and one attractive variant is the spathite, which was first identified and studied in Ozark caves. Spathites are composed of the mineral aragonite, which forms crystals that grow radially. Because of this peculiarity, spathites have a twisting or cyclic pattern of growth and often resemble a knotty soda-straw. They assume a corkscrew spiral shape that is composed of a series of superimposed "petals" that develop along the tube stem. Individual petals may be an inch or more in diameter. The tip of a spathite petal resembles the interior of a flower petal and can hold a very large drop of water.

Stalactites often begin as soda-straw structures but change to the more common carrot or icicle shape, with a thickened base and tapered stem, because the hollow tube in the center becomes plugged with mineral. When this happens, all the mineral-laden water is forced to flow down the outside of the structure. Stalactites are usually formed of calcite crystals, which grow parallel to the central canal. Irregularities in stalactite shape are common. The broader the stalactite grows at the point where it is attached to the cave ceiling, the greater its adhesive capability. This allows for the development of very large, massive stalactite groups.

Stalagmites, the counterparts of stalactites, grow up from the cave floor, usually in a gently tapered columnar or conical configuration. They are a product of the dripping water that falls from a stalactite or from the cave ceiling.

Water seldom leaves all of its mineral content overhead. When the water drop splashes and shatters upon impact, more carbon dioxide is released and calcite is

These twin soda-straws are richly stained with iron oxide. The tiny inverted images at the tips of the water drops are not reflections, but rather transmitted images from nearby soda-straws. James N. Huckins

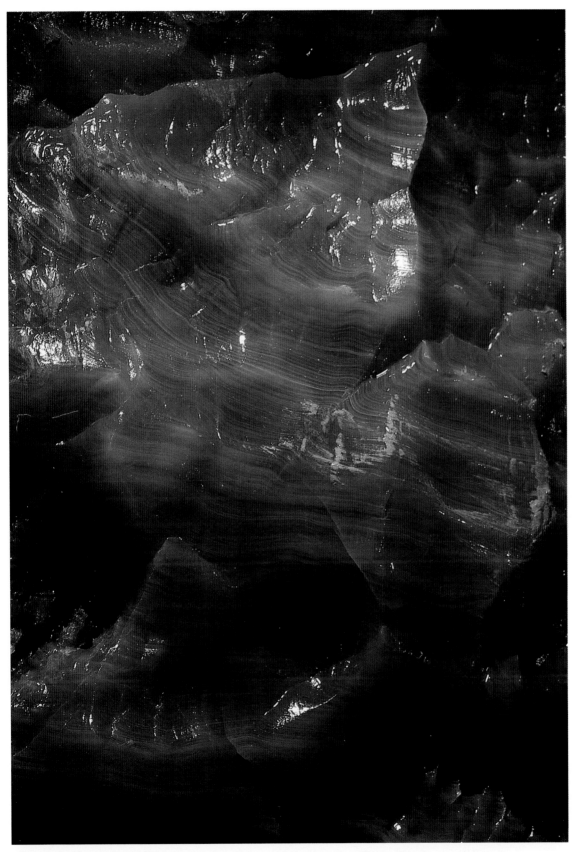

This beautiful deposit of cave onyx has been polished and scalloped by the erosive action of flowing water. Colors that highlight growth lines are caused by differences in mineral composition. James N. Huckins

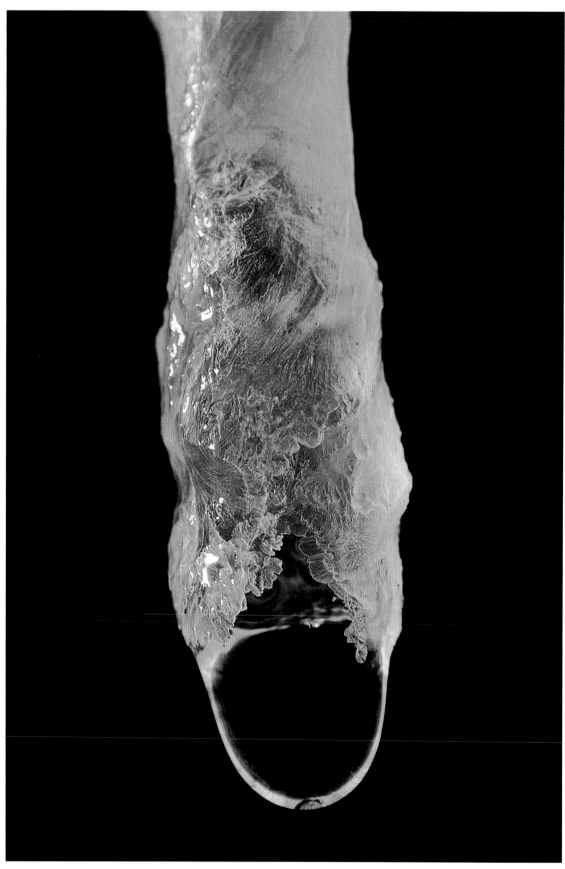

An extreme close-up of a soda-straw shows tiny crystals that have formed as the chemistry of calcite-saturated water changes with the loss of carbon dioxide. James N. Huckins

A spathite variation, similar to a soda-straw stalactite, has the appearance of a staircase.
James N. Huckins

A water drop can be seen leaving the tip of a single spathite cup in this close-up photograph. James N. Huckins

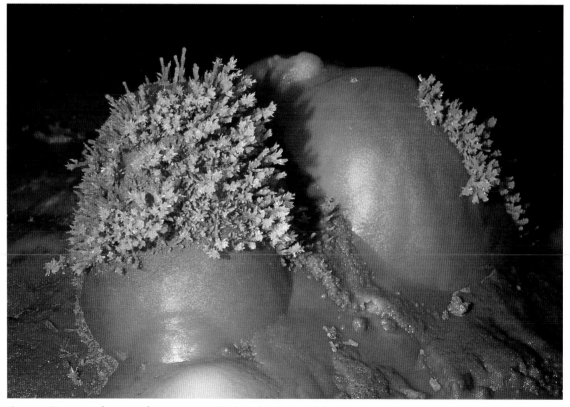

Aragonite crystals grow from unusually bright, brownish-orange stalagmites. James Vandike

precipitated. As the water flows down the sides of a stalagmite, the rippling effect of the water movement generates additional mineral deposition. Stalagmite sides often develop serrated, uneven surfaces that display shoulders and draped fringes. If the dripping water becomes undersaturated with calcite, the splashing action can dissolve the center of a stalagmite head and produce indentations called splash cups or drill holes.

Many variations of stalagmite form are possible. They may resemble Christmas trees, stools, posts, even totem poles. If a stalagmite joins with a stalactite, or reaches a ceiling on its own, a column is born. Stalagmites and columns are the giants of the dripstone family and can grow to massive size, filling an underground corridor or chamber with stately, majestic towers that may resemble the columns of some ancient temple.

Concretions, or ooliths, are an interesting type of speleothem formed by falling water drops. Concretions grow in very shallow water-filled cups, pockets, or basins on cave floors and ledges. Dripping water keeps the pool saturated with calcite. A grain of sand or some other small, unattached rock in the pool becomes the nucleus for deposition. Each time the water impacts, it agitates the pool and the grain is moved or tumbled about. Layer after layer of calcite or aragonite adheres to the grain until it becomes a rounded pebble. Irregularly shaped concretions are common. Concretions are usually white or gray, but a range of colors is possible. Concretions generally develop in "nests." As long as the water is agitated, the concretions remain loose in the nest. Without constant agitation they become cemented to the pool floor or sides.

Mineralized water flowing in thin sheets or films can coat any sloping or horizontal surface in a cave with layers of flowstone. Foreign objects lying on the cave floor in contact with the water flow can also become partially or wholly encased in layers of calcite. Flowstone has preserved the bones of ancient animals in a number of Ozark caves. Flowstone develops because water movement over rough surfaces releases carbon dioxide. If the flowstone deposit is on top of clay that is later washed away by the action of a stream, suspended canopies may result.

A drapery speleothem is another product of flowing water. Draperies or curtains of calcite develop on the surfaces of ceilings and walls, growing outward as thin undulated ribbons that may have serrated edges. A stalactite sometimes forms at the lower end where the water flow terminates. When formed of thin layers of colorless calcite, a drapery becomes a curtain of translucent stone. Generally layers of calcite alternate in color. Colorless layers alternating with reddish brown iron-rich deposits will produce a banded drape. Illuminated from behind, such curtains may resemble flags or strips of bacon.

Rimstone dams are mineral deposits that develop in the channels of shallow cave streams, on the slopes of dripstone deposits, and even on cave ledges. These dams often resemble artificial walls or rims built around a pool and are very common in Ozark caves. They grow where a stream has riffles along the cave floor due to irregularities in the streambed. The disturbances drive off carbon dioxide and release calcite. In time, a uniform flat or blade-topped wall of crystalline material develops across the stream channel. In Ozark caves rimstone dams can grow to impressive size. Dams six feet high and thirty feet wide that impound thousands of gallons of water exist in some caves. The pools behind these rimstone dams often serve as a habitat for aquatic cave life.

In a quiet cave pool that becomes heavily saturated with mineral, thin layers or patches of aragonite or calcite "ice" may form on the pool's surface. The patches of crusty calcite ice, which resemble rafts, will

Slender columns and stalagmites adorn this small grotto. Peter Chulick

Eroded, splash-cupped stalagmites grow on the floor of a cave. Jerry D. Vineyard

Glistening dripstone deposits often decorate wet cave passages. John A. Lloyd

Backlighting highlights the rich mineral staining in this large, flaglike translucent drapery.
James Glock

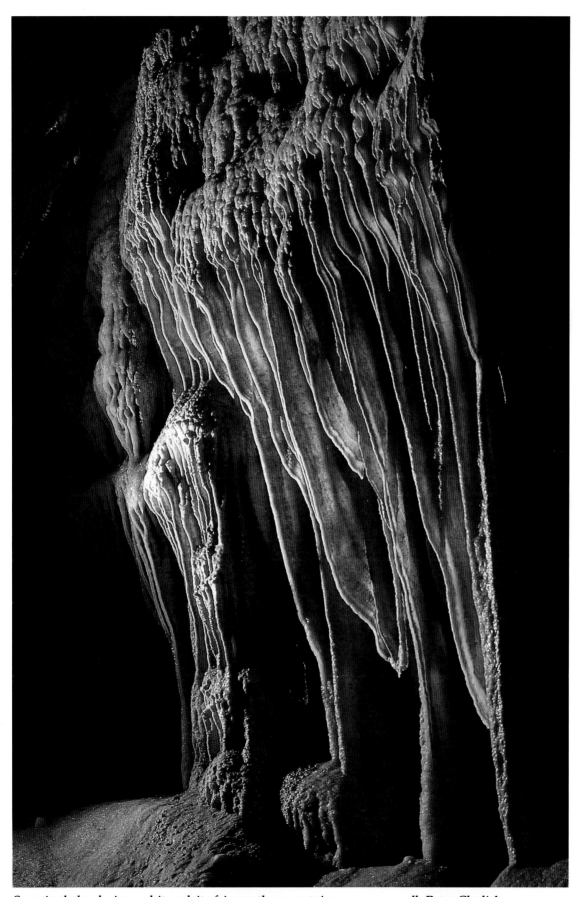

Seemingly by design, white calcite fringes these curtains on a cave wall. Peter Chulick

Shallow, crystal-clear rimstone pools cover the floor of a room in Blanchard Springs Cavern. James N. Huckins

A helictite appears to be beginning to transform into a soda-straw at its tip. James N. Huckins

Miniature and delicate, these dry crystalline rimstone dams could easily be destroyed by a misplaced step. James N. Huckins

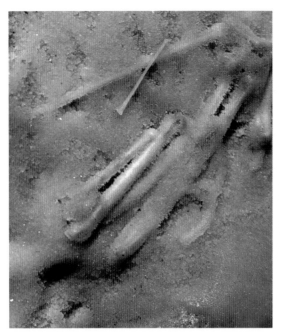

Bat bones encrusted in calcite may represent the beginning of a fossilization process.
Earl Neller

float aimlessly until water disturbance or their own weight causes them to sink. Calcite ice is normally white and very thin. If the pool dries up, the ice may become cemented to the basin walls or floor.

The seeping action of water can produce cave coral. This is a knobby mineral deposit that develops on cave walls, ceilings, floors, and even on the sides of other speleothems. It takes many globular shapes, often resembling bunches of grapes or cauliflower. In show caves such deposits are often referred to as cave popcorn. Coral forms that develop through seepage appear to be the most common types in Ozark caves, but variations that grow underwater through a concretion process and types that form at the base of stalagmites through a splash process also exist.

Helictites are the contortionists of the speleothem family. The word *helictite* comes from the Greek word *helix*, which means "to spiral"; however, helictites exhibit many shapes in addition to a helix. Helictites should not be confused with spathites. Spathites may corkscrew and twist along

the stem, but they are generally restricted to cave ceilings and resemble knotty soda-straws. Helictites are usually wiry and rootlike; they are formed by seeping water and can grow in clusters almost anywhere in a cave from floor to ceiling. Numerous theories have been advanced to explain their bizarre growth style. The favored one suggests that hydrostatic pressure forces a tiny amount of water from the cavernous bedrock, and precipitation of the carbonate mineral occurs where the water emerges in the cave. As the tiny tube lengthens, water pressure, along with variations in crystallization of the carbonate minerals, causes an eccentric growth pattern.

Gypsum is the floral arranger of the Ozark cave world. It is a hydrous sulfate mineral that can form distinctive, colorless crystals (a variety called selenite) or white, silky, fibrous extrusions. Gypsum may appear in many shapes, but the ones most common to the caves of the Ozark Plateau include needles, hair, crust, and flowers.

Selenite needles are formed when gypsum leached from the soil by the wicking action of water crystallizes in the direction of least resistance. This is usually upward, away from the cave floor. The needles normally form in clusters. Irregularities in crystal growth will occasionally produce curved needles, but they are rare. Selenite needles are so delicate and fragile that they can be broken by the shock wave of a loud sound, the impact of the human breath, the heat of a carbide light, or even the lightest touch.

Gypsum hair, resembling fibrous threads, grows from cave ceilings or ledges and takes the shape of twisted strands or beards. Cave hair may develop along a bedrock fracture where the gypsum threads grow out in the line of least resistance. Gypsum hair deposits, like gypsum needles, are extremely fragile.

Gypsum flowers are among the most beautiful of all speleothems because of their silky luster, symmetry, and flowerlike

An elfin-like helictite forest grows from the floor of a small chamber. Terry Pitchford

A large selenite needle display on a sandy cave floor is almost invisible unless backlit. Cavers must carefully traverse around such growths to preserve their fragile beauty. James N. Huckins

This gypsum flake extending from the ceiling of a cave is an example of the processes of growth and exfoliation. Rickard L. Walk

This small curved needle is atypical, since most selenite needles are linear. James Glock

A long gypsum curl speleothem, measuring approximately nine inches, has longitudinal lines delineating crystal fibers. James N. Huckins

Delicate helictites, in seeming defiance of gravity, exist in a remarkable variety of shapes.
Rickard L. Walk

nature. Like needles and hair, they have an extrusive growth pattern—they are formed of fibrous crystal aggregates that grow outward from cave walls, ceilings, and ledges. Growth is most rapid at the center of the flower cluster, causing the petal extrusions to curve outward in a radial pattern. Clusters can become relatively large with individual petals several inches wide and about twelve inches in length.

Speleothems brighten the subterranean world of solitude and brooding darkness. They accent drab walls, floors, and ceilings and create illusions. They give compositional coherence through repetition of lines, colors, and shapes. In a sculpted cavescape containing sediments strewn with bedrock masses, speleothems catch the eye. They appear as an outward expression of remarkable internal order and provide refinement to a grotto.

Underground compositions of rocks, sediments, and crystal deposits are three-dimensional works of natural art in which the observer becomes more than a disengaged viewer. The cave and its elaborate hierarchy of forms envelop the observer on all sides. Aesthetic detachment is often not possible, which is one reason caves have such an impact upon the human spirit. These compositions take thousands or even hundreds of thousands of years to develop. Many of the speleothem components can be destroyed in an instant by human carelessness. Such destruction may last forever.

Ozark Cave Life

The caves of the Ozark Plateau are places where man can encounter life-forms from the stygian realms of the underground wilderness network. A human can explore a cave only as far as the shape and size of the body permit. Beyond that lie corridors of labyrinthine extent that mankind will never see, chart, or fully comprehend. Every explorable cave and spring is linked to this kingdom of total darkness—the interstitial heart of the Ozark bedrock.

The interstitial zone consists primarily of the small spaces among particles of rock or soil, but it also encompasses a network of solutional cavities and enlarged underground channels linked vertically and horizontally by fractures in the thick layers of Ozark limestone and dolomite. Most of these secondary cavities and channels are too small for human passage, but they are home to many species of life. The invertebrates include worms, leeches, snails, isopods, amphipods, crayfish, flies, pseudoscorpions, crickets, beetles, fleas, spiders,

In the twilight zone, hidden from casual observers, a pickerel frog (*Rana palustris*) sits in a solution pocket of a cave wall. Rickard L. Walk

millipedes, and springtails. Vertebrates include mammals, fishes, reptiles, and amphibians.

Explorable caves, which can be considered the largest portions of the secondary interstitial zone, are separated from surface ecosystems, yet cave life is highly dependent on energy input from the outside world. Predator, prey, and scavenger all live in balance, but that balance can be quickly destroyed by the impact of human activity. Many types of life-forms are highly vulnerable to waterborne pollutants that can reach them through sinkholes, sinking streams, abandoned mines, and improperly constructed water wells. Even underground storage tanks can pollute the interstitial zone.

In November 1981, an estimated 80,000 liters of liquid ammonium nitrate and urea fertilizer spilled from a pipeline near Dry Fork Creek in the Missouri Ozarks. This sinking stream feeds part of the Maramec Spring watershed in Phelps County. Maramec Spring is one of the large springs of the Salem Plateau and has an average daily discharge of 93 million gallons.

The liquid ammonium nitrate took seven days to reach the spring outlet through the interstitial network in the spring's aquifer. It killed 37,000 trout at a hatchery operated near the mouth of the spring. For more than a month the ammonium nitrate concentration remained high in the water, killing and injuring aquatic underground species that included the rare Salem cave crayfish (*Cambarus hubrichti*) and the southern cave-fish (*Typhlichthys subterraneus*). The pollution is estimated to have killed 10,000 Salem cave crayfish; in addition, nearly 1,000 of the rare southern cave-fish surfaced at the spring and were seriously affected by the ammonium nitrate. The spill also led to the death of many grotto salamanders (*Typhlotriton spelaeus*).

This incident graphically documents the link between the surface environment in which we live and the subterranean environment in which life-forms of the underground wilderness live. These organisms are sentinels of pollution stress, and their continued existence, and ours, depends upon high-quality groundwater. Ozark springs are linked to the interstitial zone and are simply water-filled caves. The protection of caves and their contents, whether living or inorganic, is therefore ultimately linked to our own well-being.

Zones of Cave Life

In general, an Ozark cave can be divided into three types of habitats—the entrance zone of sunlight and shade, the twilight zone of eerie shadows and dim light, and the zone of complete darkness. This type of segregation is used for descriptive purposes only, as numerous species of cave life can survive in more than one zone.

Biologists classify species of animals found in caves into three general categories based on their life histories or their adaptation to caves. Troglobites are animals that spend their entire life cycle in caves and cannot survive outside. Endemic Ozark blind cave-fish and crayfish are well known troglobitic species. Trogloxenes are animals that use caves or cavelike environments during part of their life cycle, but they also live in and depend on the outside environment for their survival. The gray bat and the Herald moth are examples of this type of animal. Troglophiles are animals that can survive both in caves and in some outside environments but generally prefer caves. The amphipod *Gammarus minus*, the pickerel frog, and cave crickets are common troglophiles.

Most animals frequenting the entrance area of a cave are surface dwellers that usually don't venture into the zone of total darkness because of its lack of food and light and its constant low temperature. Cave-visiting raccoons and cave-loving crickets are exceptions, and they can be

The non-pigmented grotto salamander larva (*Typhlotriton spelaeus*) has an external gill structure. Eugene Vale

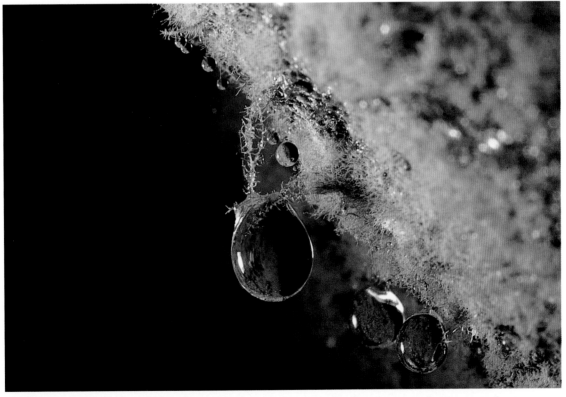

Tiny dewdrops provide life-sustaining moisture for moss in the photosynthetic zone of a cave entrance passage. James N. Huckins

found in all three life zones. Amphibians, reptiles, mollusks, insects, and mammals are all represented among the cave-entrance dwellers. Eastern phoebes also nest in Ozark cave openings. The entrance chamber protects these animals from the harshest extremes of weather.

The range of the twilight zone is determined by the size and shape of the cave's entrance corridor. The twilight zone usually begins just inside the entrance and ends where total darkness begins. The twilight zone is an area of variable temperatures that may change from 70°F in the summer to 3°F in the winter. The variable air temperatures of this zone usually extend into the dark zone for a short distance. If the twilight zone carries a stream from the cave's interior, the water temperature generally changes gradually from the constant temperature of the dark zone as it leaves the cave.

The twilight zone is a transition area between two types of habitats. Creatures who are often found in the twilight zone are species that have adapted to its cloak of shadows and moderately variable temperatures. Various species of salamanders, frogs, insects, crustaceans, and mammals use the twilight zone. Cave crickets, cave beetles, harvestman spiders, and bats traffic the twilight of the entrance corridor.

In the zone of total darkness the temperatures of air, water, and rock are usually the same and are relatively constant throughout the year. A cave's temperature approximates the mean annual temperature of the cave's geographical location, which is controlled by its latitude and its altitude above sea level. For caves in the northern half of the Ozarks, the temperature is about 56°F. Caves in the southern half are closer to 60°F.

Troglobites usually live in the zone of total darkness. However, some troglobites such as the bristly cave crayfish (*Cambarus setosus*) can live successfully in all three zones. The number of species generally

found in the zone of total darkness is substantial but still limited when compared to the number of species usually present in the twilight zone and outside habitats. Animals commonly found in the zone of total darkness include blind and unpigmented salamanders, fish, crayfish, amphipods, isopods, millipedes, and beetles.

A large percentage of troglobitic cave animals are omnivorous. Their nourishment comes from two primary sources—it is imported from the outside by species of trogloxenes, troglophiles, and cave visitors in the form of feces or the bodies of deceased cave animals (primarily bats, raccoons, pack rats, and crickets), or it is made up of debris washed into the cave by runoff and wet-weather streams.

The process that leads to unpigmented skin and blindness in troglobitic species is evolutionary in nature, requiring many generations of reproduction in the dark zone. In their quest for survival, the blind, unpigmented animals are aided by body adaptations that give them advantages. The grotto salamander, for instance, has a slim body and very sensitive vibration sensors that are important for locating and reaching food. The blind cave-fish has excellent balance, long fins for smooth swimming, and a large head with highly developed odor-perception centers, vibration sensors, and a large short-term memory center.

In some caves evolutionary changes have resulted in species of cave life restricted to one site only. The Tumbling Creek Cave Snail found in the cave where the Ozark Underground Laboratory is located and the pink planarian at Rock Bridge Memorial State Park in the Missouri Ozarks are examples of these rare life-forms.

The blind and fragile life-forms that dwell in the underground wilderness are generally limited in number and distribution and represent many generations of evolutionary adaptation. They often cannot survive outside their own special ecosystems.

In many caves, the camel cave cricket (*Ceuthophilus*) is the most common member of the invertebrate population. Rickard L. Walk.

A translucent bristly cave crayfish (*Cambarus setosus*) sits in its cave-stream habitat. Richard Thom

Fungus gnat larva (*Macrocera nobilis*) are the architects of delicate web structures in some caves.
Robert L. Taylor

Small cave isopods (*Caecidotea*) feed on organic matter in a shallow pool. James N. Huckins

A creature of complete darkness, this Ozark blind cave-fish (*Amblyopsis rosae*) was found in Fantastic Caverns, Missouri. Cave organisms such as this blind fish are highly susceptible to groundwater pollution. Robert L. Taylor

The endangered pink planarian (*Macrocotyla glandulosa*), less than one inch long, is an aquatic invertebrate found only in Devil's Icebox, Rock Bridge Memorial State Park, Missouri. Scott Schulte

Bats

Bats have been around for 60 million years and probably have been using caves for much of that time. They roost in caves during the daytime, finding places to rest in either the twilight zone or the zone of total darkness. During the warm months of the year they leave caves at night to feed. Caves also serve as nurseries for rearing their young, and as hibernacula for the winter months.

Legend, superstition, fiction, film, and human ignorance have not been kind to bats. Contrary to what many people think, bats are actually shy, harmless, beneficial animals that are important to the balance of nature.

At least thirteen species of bats live in the Ozarks, and nine of them frequent caves. These species include the endan-gered gray bat (*Myotis grisescens*), the endangered Indiana bat (*Myotis sodalis*), the little brown bat (*Myotis lucifugus*), the small-footed bat (*Myotis leibii*), the big brown bat (*Eptesicus fuscus*), the eastern pipistrelle bat (*Pipistrellus subflavus*), the Keen's bat (*Myotis keenii*), the eastern big-eared bat (*Plecotus rafinesquii*), and the endangered Ozark big-eared bat (*Plecotus townsendii ingens*).

Ozark bats hunt their prey at night when the moths, mosquitoes, and other small insects that they eat are flying about in large numbers. Bats eat enormous numbers of these insect pests. The darkness also helps protect the bats from predators such as owls and hawks. Bats are not blind; they see quite well, but nature has also gifted them with echo location. They produce ultrasonic cries that reflect from solid objects and return as echoes to their sensitive ears. This enables them to navigate in the dark without striking objects and aids them in catching their tiny, flying prey.

Bat droppings beneath roosts create thick mats or piles of guano. These droppings, which consist largely of undigested insect parts, are an important food source for other forms of cave life. The guano attracts cave scavengers and decomposers who in turn become food for each other. Thus bats, and especially their guano, are often the basis of the food chain in a cave. Bats are so important to the ecosystem of some caves that their disappearance would cause a breakdown in the food chain of those caves.

The actions of man are the primary cause of endangered bat species in the Ozarks. Human disturbance and the poisoning with pesticides of the insects the bats feed on are thought to be the major reasons for declines in bat populations. Only through understanding of the importance of bats can these fascinating animals be conserved as a key part of the underground wilderness.

A solitary eastern pipistrelle bat (*Pipistrellus subflavus*) wears a coat of dewdrops. Human disturbance of bats during some seasons and early life stages could be fatal to these beneficial mammals. Rickard L. Walk

The endangered gray bat (*Myotis grisescens*) in flight is an efficient predator of insect pests. Merlin D. Tuttle

Animal Graveyards

Preserved remains of animal species both surviving and extinct are frequently found in Ozark caves. Over the past three decades, vertebrate paleontologists have cataloged thousands of individual pieces that represent more than 850 species. These remains are an important resource for evaluating Ozark animal life and climate from the Late Pleistocene epoch, which marked the end of the ice age over 10,000 years ago, until today.

Many animals now extinct roamed the wilderness regions of the Ozark Plateau when the nomadic ancestors of the American Indian appeared 12,000 years ago. These animals included the long-legged Dire wolf, American lion, jaguar, flat-headed peccary, saber-toothed cat, ground sloth, elk, bison, mastodon, mammoth, and several species of bear. Today, bones, teeth, footprints, and claw marks of some of these animals are found in the dark solitude of Ozark caves appearing just as they were entombed 8,000 to 30,000 years ago.

Animals such as the bison, elk, and mastodon did not frequent caves. But their bones were carried into caves by predators and storm waters. Caves with pit openings also served as natural traps from which animals usually could not escape if they fell in. The bones and teeth of these animals are generally found in cave gravel, silt, and clay sediments.

Jaguars (*Panthera onca*), saber-toothed cats (*Smilodon* sp.), and American lions (*Panthera leo atrox*) probably denned in cave openings. In one Missouri Ozark cave where the clear footprints of a cat are preserved in flowstone-covered clay, the cat tracks can be followed through the cave passage for three-quarters of a mile. The trail also indicates the presence of a second, smaller cat.

The most recently discovered cat tracks are in another Missouri Ozark cave. They are the footprints of the American lion. Each pad print in undisturbed clay is 7$^{1}/_{2}$ inches wide. These are the largest Pleistocene cat tracks yet discovered in a North American cave. It is estimated that the big cat stood 48 inches high at the shoulder, weighed about 900 pounds at maturity, and became extinct approximately 8,000 years ago.

Black bears (*Ursus americanus*) and the extinct giant short-faced bear (*Arctotherium* sp.) used Ozark caves as quarters for their winter sleep. Thousands of their old craterlike wallows and beds dimple the clay banks and clay floors of Ozark caves. The marks of bear claws, some preserved in flowstone, are still visible on Ozark cave walls and clay banks.

Cavers who find bone deposits or unusual tracks should leave them undisturbed and carefully note their location in the cave. That information should be passed on to the Division of Geology and Land Survey of the Missouri Department of Natural Resources in Rolla.

This paw print of the extinct American lion (*Panthera leo atrox*) in cave clay is estimated to be eight thousand years old. It measures seven and a half inches across. James Vandike

These anthodite clusters appear to be pure aragonite. This type of crystalline form is not common in Ozark caves. James N. Huckins

Sunless Sanctuaries

The caves of the Ozark Plateau are sunless sanctuaries for many threatened and endangered species of animal life. They are natural museums that house ancient structures of rock and crystal where millions of years of geological history can unfold before human eyes. They house spectacular scenery that can be found nowhere else in the Ozarks. They are the burial grounds of archaeological and paleontological history, places of unique spiritual enrichment, and crucibles for scientific discovery.

The wild caves of the Ozarks are threatened by surface development that strips away forest and soil cover. They are being overrun by residential, commercial, and industrial sprawl. The water that gives them shape and life is being contaminated by man. The caves are victims of careless recreational activity, and they are being damaged by too much human intrusion into the underground wilderness. The sculptured rock forms and speleothems found in Ozark caves are nonrenewable and irreplaceable. Once damaged, they are damaged forever in our comprehension because they represent thousands or even millions of years of geological development.

Caves are the last real wilderness left in the Ozarks. They are special places—sanctuaries of all the qualities that define true underground wilderness and underground beauty. Underground wilderness is silence and solitude that frees a person from the distractions of a busy, troubled world. It is a spiritual sanctuary. Those who seek the uninhabited wilderness refuge of caves, whether for recreation or for scientific information, find the experience physically and emotionally uplifting.

Underground wilderness is felt in the wet chill and damp that penetrate clothing and in the endless stretches of deep mud and sticky clay. It is embodied in mountains of breakdown that must be laboriously scaled, icy cave streams to be forded, and the conquest of seemingly bottomless pitches whose depths are shrouded in darkness. It is experienced through coming to grips with the reality of darkness that fills every chamber, corridor, nook, and cranny in the cave.

Underground wilderness is the eerie darkness at the edge of the twilight zone that promises discovery. It exists in the gentle flutter of bats on the wing, in the ghostly dartings of blind fish in a cave stream, and in the lovely dark eyes and bright orange and black coats of cave salamanders glistening with moisture in the illumination of an explorer's light. It is the glimmer in the dewy moisture on the fur of a hibernating bat, and the slow back-and-forth motion of the long, elegant antennae of watchful cave crickets.

Underground wilderness is the chatter of a cave stream and the roar and thunder of a subterranean waterfall. It takes your breath away as you stand witness to the towering majesty of a giant dome or the

The giant columns and stalagmites known as "The Titans" in Blanchard Springs Cavern are in the "wild" part of the cave. James Glock

The pristine beauty of this cathedral-like chamber can easily be marred by careless visitors. John A. Lloyd

The colorful adult cave salamander (*Eurycea lucifuga*) is found in many Ozark caves. Eugene Vale

quiet glassy surface of an underground lake. It lurks in the absence of all things familiar.

Underground wilderness is the serenity of a crystal-rimmed pool, the fragility of helictites, the daintiness of soda-straw stalactites, the glassy qualities of water drops clinging to the tips of speleothems, and the astonishing blend of subtle colors that highlight mineral deposits.

The wise use and preservation of the underground wilderness of the Ozark Plateau now will assure that this wonderful resource survives for all future generations.

A spacious and cool entrance gallery streaked with white mineral deposits entices weary hikers to rest. Rickard L. Walk

Glossary

The definitions of these terms are for the most part specific to their use in describing caves. They are not generic in scope.

Aerated zone: an area between the surface of the ground and the water table where the pore spaces of soil and rock formations are mostly filled with air; also called the vadose zone.

Anthodite: a speleothem consisting of radial clusters of needles or quill-like crystals, often composed of aragonite.

Aquifer: a layer or layers of permeable rock, sand, or other formations that can store and yield usable amounts of groundwater.

Aragonite: a mineral composed of calcium carbonate, usually in the form of needle-like crystals but also found in other speleothem forms; has a different crystal habit from calcite.

Artesian water: groundwater under sufficient hydrostatic pressure to rise above the aquifer containing it.

Bedding plane: the dividing line or fracture that separates two layers of stratified rock; where two different layers of horizontal rock meet.

Bedrock: solid rock beneath the soil.

Botryoid: a speleothem shaped like a bunch of grapes or cauliflower; also called cave coral.

Breakdown: single blocks or piles of rocks and boulders that have fallen from the ceiling or walls of a cave during its development stages or later.

Calcite: a common cave mineral that forms most speleothems; composed of calcium carbonate; the primary cementing mineral in limestone; has a different crystal habit from aragonite.

Canopy: an overhang of flowstone.

Carbonic acid: the weak acid (H_2CO_3) resulting from interaction of carbon dioxide and water.

Cave: a natural underground opening permitting human entry, usually formed in rock by the dissolving action of acidic groundwater.

Cave coral: a speleothem with branching stems and nodular tips that resembles cauliflower or bunches of grapes. Also called botryoid.

Caver: a person who explores caves.

Cavern: same as a cave.

Chert: a sedimentary rock composed of fine-grained quartz and resembling flint.

Column: a speleothem formed by the union of a stalactite and a stalagmite, or a speleothem connected to both the ceiling and the floor.

Commercial cave: a cave with an admission charge; a cave prepared for public visitation; a cave with trails and guides; same as a show cave.

Concretion: a carbonate speleothem, often spheroidal or ellipsoidal in shape, which may form in a shallow cave pool; an oolith or cave pearl.

Dolomite: a sedimentary rock similar to limestone, largely or completely composed of the mineral calcium-magnesium carbonate.

Dome: a cylindrical natural shaft or chimney in a cave ceiling.

This cave has a skylight to the outer world. Robert Glock

Domepit: a cylindrical natural shaft that passes through a cave passage with a dome in the ceiling directly over a pit in the floor.

Dripstone: any speleothem formed through the action of dripping water.

Endemic: native to a particular area or cave.

Epsomite: a rare and very water-soluble hydrous magnesium sulfate cave mineral.

Erosion: the gradual wearing away, deterioration, and disintegration of rock or sediments by running water.

Flowstone: a sheetlike or ice flow–like speleothem formed by films of moving water.

Formation: a unit of bedrock; a word often loosely and inappropriately used, as in the phrase *cave formations*, to describe speleothems.

Fossiliferous rock: a sedimentary rock formation that contains an abundance of fossils.

Fracture: *see* Joint.

Geomorphology: the science dealing with the nature and origin of the earth's topographic features.

Groundwater: water below the surface of the earth.

Guano: the solid waste of bats.

Gypsum: a sedimentary rock or mineral composed of hydrous calcium sulfate, softer and more soluble than limestone.

Gypsum crust: a gypsum deposit that forms on some cave walls.

Gypsum flower: a speleothem formed of gypsum that resembles a flower blossom with outwardly curved, radial petals with longitudinal lines.

Gypsum hair: a speleothem made of hydrous calcium sulfate that resembles whiskers or hair.

Helictite: a small, twisted, rootlike or wormlike speleothem composed of calcite or aragonite that appears to grow in defiance of the law of gravity.

Igneous formation: rock or mineral, such as lava or basalt, that solidified from cooled molten rock or magma.

Interstitial zone: the small spaces among particles of rock or soil; the network of solutional cavities and enlarged underground channels linked vertically and horizontally by fractures in the sedimentary bedrock.

Joint: a natural crack or fracture in rock not accompanied by dislocation.

Karst: a landscape characterized by the presence of sinkholes, caves, springs, and losing or disappearing streams created as groundwater dissolves sedimentary rock such as limestone.

Limestone: a sedimentary rock largely or completely composed of calcium carbonate; a rock of marine origin derived from lime mud and ooze that accumulated on calm, shallow sea floors.

Losing stream: a stream in a karst region that loses a significant amount of its flow to the ground; a stream that disappears underground; a sinking stream.

Meandering niche: a notch or recessed opening incised into the rock wall of a cave by the cutting action of a stream.

Meandering stream: a sinuous stream that winds in an intricate course.

Mirabilite: a rare and very soluble hydrous sodium sulfate cave mineral.

Natural bridge: a natural arch or span of rock left standing after the collapse of a cave passage; a karst feature caused by the dissolving action of water and by abrasion from water-borne sediments.

Oolith: *see* Concretion.

Oxides: minerals characterized by the linking of oxygen atoms with a metallic element.

Paleontology: the branch of geology that deals with life-forms from the past, especially prehistoric life-forms, through the study of plant and animal fossils.

Pendant: a hanging projection of bedrock; a speleogen, as opposed to a speleothem.

Permeable formation: a fractured or porous layer of rock that will allow water to move through it.

Phreatic zone: *see* Water-saturated zone.

Pit: a vertical shaft in the floor of a cave; a cave with a vertical entrance that may require climbing gear.

Pollutant: any substance that degrades the quality of the environment.

Porosity: the volume of spaces within a material relative to the volume of its solid mass; the ability of a formation to absorb and store groundwater; porousness.

Recharge: the process of water moving from the surface down to the water table; the process of adding to the supply of groundwater.

Rimstone dam: a speleothem that consists of a mineral rim around a cave pool or a dam across a streambed; often found as a dry crystalline structure due to changes in hydrologic conditions.

Saltpeter: the nitrate salts of calcium, formerly used in making gunpowder.

Scallop: an unsymmetrical eroded depression or shallow bowl caused by stream action on cave walls or on speleothems.

Sediments: material borne and deposited by water.

Selenite: a coarsely crystalline, transparent variety of gypsum.

Show cave: the preferred term for a commercial cave.

Silica: silicon dioxide occurring as crystalline quartz.

Sinkhole: a bowl-shaped depression in the ground or a truncated hollow associated with karst topography and caves; a natural depression in the ground that collects water and funnels it underground.

Solution: the act or process of acidic water dissolving the soluble mineral content of the rock and causing it to break up, change shape, or be dispelled or dissipated.

Spar, dogtooth: calcite crystals that resemble teeth.

Spathite: an aragonite speleothem consisting of a vertical succession of small petal-shaped, thin-walled cones; a corkscrew-shaped speleothem.

This strikingly weathered rock, which resembles petrified wood, was shaped by the action of a cave stream. James N. Huckins

This decorated chamber formed where porous dolomite and sandstone layers met.
James N. Huckins

Speleogen: a cave feature formed by solution, perhaps assisted by abrasion from waterborne sediments.

Speleogenesis: the origin and development of caves and their associated features.

Speleology: the study or science of caves.

Speleothem: a secondary mineral deposit formed in caves; the preferred term for a cave formation.

Spelunker: same as a caver.

Spongework: cavities in rock that resemble spaces in a sponge on a larger scale; honeycomb-like cavities produced by solution.

Stalactite: a speleothem that hangs from a cave ceiling, formed by dripping water.

Stalagmite: a speleothem that grows up from the floor of a cave, formed by water dripping from above.

Stygian: unlighted, dark, gloomy, subterranean.

Troglobite: an animal that spends its entire life cycle in caves and cannot survive outside; cave dweller.

Troglodyte: a nonspecific term for a cave dweller, human or otherwise.

Troglophile: an animal that can survive in both caves and some outside environments but generally prefers caves; cave lover.

Trogloxene: an animal that uses caves or cavelike environments during part of its life cycle but lives in the outside environment the rest of the time; a cave guest.

Vadose zone: *see* Aerated zone.

Water-saturated zone: a level below the ground where all pore spaces are water filled; below the water table; also called the phreatic zone.

Watershed: the total land area that supplies water to a cave or a spring.

Water table: the surface or top level of the water-saturated zone.

Weathering: the wearing away of rock and soil through natural chemical and physical processes.

Wild cave: a cave that has not been commercialized.

A variety of speleothems grace this large passage. Robert L. Taylor

Bibliography

Abercrombie, Stanley. *Architecture as Art.* New York: Van Nostrand Reinhold Co., 1984. 176 pp.

Barbour, Roger W., and Wayne H. Davis. *Bats of America.* Lexington: University Press of Kentucky, 1969. 286 pp.

Bates, Robert L., and Julia A. Jackson. *Dictionary of Geological Terms.* Garden City: Anchor Press/Doubleday, 1976. 571 pp.

Beveridge, Thomas R. *Geologic Wonders and Curiosities of Missouri.* Rolla: Missouri Department of Natural Resources, Division of Geology and Land Survey, 1978. 453 pp.

Boorstin, Daniel J. *The Exploring Spirit.* New York: Random House, 1976. 102 pp.

Bretz, J. Harlen. *Caves of Missouri.* Rolla: Missouri Department of Business and Administration, Division of Geological Survey and Water Resources, 1956. 491 pp.

———. "Excerpts from the 'Memories of J. Harlen Bretz.'" With commentary by Jerry D. Vineyard. *Missouri Speleology* 19:3–4 (1979): 69 pp.

———. *Geomorphic History of the Ozarks of Missouri.* Rolla: Missouri Department of Business and Administration, Division of Geological Survey and Water Resources, 1965. 147 pp.

———. "Vadose and Phreatic Features of Limestone Caverns." *Journal of Geology* 50 (1942): 675–811.

Brucker, Roger W. "Caves and Cavers: An Overview." In *National Cave Management Symposium Proceedings,* 2–5. Albuquerque: Speleobooks, 1976.

Brucker, Roger W., and Richard Watson. *The Longest Cave.* Carbondale: Southern Illinois University Press, 1976. 331 pp.

Courbon, Paul, and Claude Chabert. *Atlas of the Great Caves of the World.* St. Louis: Cave Books, 1989. 369 pp.

Crunkilton, Ronald. "Subterranean Contamination of Meramec Spring by Ammonium Nitrate and Urea Fertilizer and Its Implication on Rare Cave Biota." In *Proceedings of the 1984 National Cave Management Symposium,* 151–58. *Missouri Speleology* 25:1–4 (1985): 236 pp.

Culver, David. *Cave Life: Evolution and Ecology.* Cambridge: Harvard University Press, 1982. 189 pp.

Dickinson, Leo. *Cave Diving: The Caving Diving Group Manual.* Somerset, Eng.: Mendip Publishing, 1990. 268 pp.

Dougherty, Percy. *Environmental Karst.* Cincinnati: GeoSpeleo Publications, 1983. 167 pp.

Exley, Sheck. *Basic Cave Diving: A Blueprint for Survival.* Branford, Fla.: National Speleological Society, 1986. 46 pp.

Fact Sheet on Bats. Jefferson City: Missouri Department of Conservation, 1980.

Ford, Derek, and Paul Williams. *Karst Geomorphology and Hydrology.* London, Eng.: Unwin Hyman, 1989. 601 pp.

Fuller, Michael J. "Caves, Rockshelters, and Prehistoric Indians in the Ozarks." In *Speleology Workshop Manual,* 53–66. Springfield: Southwest Missouri State University, 1980.

Gans, Roma. *Caves.* New York: Thomas Y. Crowell Co., 1976. 33 pp.

Gardner, James E. *Invertebrate Fauna from Missouri Caves and Springs.* Jefferson City: Missouri Department of Conservation, 1986. 72 pp.

Ground-Water Protection Curriculum Guide. Jefferson City: Missouri Department of Natural Resources, 1989. 52 pp.

Dewdrops cover a moth (*Scoliopteryx libatrix*) near a cave entrance. Bruce Schuette

Gurnee, Russell and Jeanne. *Gurnee Guide to American Caves*. Closter, N.J.: R. H. Gurnee, 1990. 288 pp.

Halliday, William R. *American Caves and Caving*. New York: Harper & Row, 1974. 348 pp.

———. *Depths of the Earth*. New York: Harper & Row, 1966. 398 pp.

Hawksley, Oscar. *Missouri Ozark Waterways*. Jefferson City: Missouri Department of Conservation, 1976. 114 pp.

———. "Remains of Quaternary Vertebrates from Ozark Caves and Miscellaneous Sites." *Missouri Speleology* 26:1–2 (1986): 1–67.

Hill, Carol A., and Paolo Forti. *Cave Minerals of the World*. Huntsville: National Speleological Society, 1986. 238 pp.

Hines, John and Molly. *The Secret World of Bats*. London: Methuen Children's Books, 1986. 64 pp.

Howes, Chris. *Cave Photography: A Practical Guide*. Buxton, Eng.: Caving Supplies, 1987. 68 pp.

———. *To Photograph Darkness: The History of Underground and Flash Photography*. Carbondale: Southern Illinois University Press, 1989. 330 pp.

Hudson, Steve, ed. *Manual of U.S. Cave Rescue Techniques*. Huntsville: National Speleological Society, 1988. 260 pp.

Jackson, Donald Dale. *Underground Worlds*. Alexandria: Time-Life Books, 1982. 176 pp.

Jennings, J. N. *Karst*. Cambridge: The MIT Press, 1971. 252 pp.

———. *Karst Geomorphology*. New York: Basil Blackwell, 1985. 293 pp.

Johnson, Sylvia A. *The World of Bats*. Minneapolis: Learner Publications Co., 1985. 48 pp.

Johnson, Tom R. "Family Plethodontidae." In *The Amphibians and Reptiles of Missouri*, 66–88. Jefferson City: Missouri Department of Conservation, 1987.

Keller, W. D. *Common Rocks and Minerals of Missouri*. Columbia: University of Missouri Press, 1973. 78 pp.

Kerbo, Ronal C. *Caves*. Chicago: Children's Press, 1981. 48 pp.

Kurten, Bjorn. *The Cave Bear Story*. New York: Columbia University Press, 1976. 163 pp.

Lavaur, Guy de. *Caves and Cave Diving*. New York: Crown Publishers, 1956. 175 pp.

Lawrence, Joe, Jr., and Roger W. Brucker. *The Caves Beyond: The Story of the Floyd Collins Crystal Cave Exploration*. St. Louis: Cave Books, 1975. 318 pp.

McClurg, David. *Adventure of Caving*. Carlsbad: D. & J. Press, 1986. 332 pp.

————. *Exploring Caves*. Harrisburg: Stackpole Books, 1975. 288 pp.

McReynolds, H. E. "Rare and Endangered Cave Animals." In *National Cave Management Symposium Proceedings*, 39–42. Albuquerque: Speleobooks, 1976.

Mehl, M. G. *Missouri's Ice Age Animals*. Rolla: Missouri Department of Business and Administration, Division of Geological Survey and Water Resources, 1962. 104 pp.

Missouri's Hidden Waters. Jefferson City: Missouri Department of Natural Resources, 1987. 8 pp.

Moore, Charles E., and Thomas L. Poulson. *The Life of the Cave*. New York: McGraw-Hill Book Co., 1966. 232 pp.

Moore, Charles W., and G. Nicholas Sullivan. *Speleology: The Study of Caves*. St. Louis: Cave Books, 1981. 150 pp.

Murray, Robert K., and Roger W. Brucker. *Trapped*. Lexington: University Press of Kentucky, 1979. 335 pp.

Naken, C. J. *I Can Read about Caves*. Mahwah, N.J.: Troll Associates, 1979. 44 pp.

"Origin of Limestone Caves." *Bulletin of the National Speleological Society* 22:1 (1960): 1–84.

Owen, Luella Agnes. "Excerpts from *Cave Regions of Ozarks and Black Hills of South Dakota, 1898*." *Missouri Speleology* 10:2 (1968): 22–86.

Padgett, Allen, and Bruce Smith. *On Rope*. Huntsville: National Speleological Society, 1987. 341 pp.

Price, Michael. *Introducing Groundwater*. Winchester, Me.: George Allen & Unwin, 1985. 195 pp.

Rafferty, Milton D. *The Ozarks Land and Life*. Norman: University of Oklahoma Press, 1980. 282 pp.

Rea, Tom, ed. *Caving Basics*. Huntsville: National Speleological Society, 1987. 128 pp.

Rhodes, Richard. *The Ozarks*. New York: Time-Life Books, 1974. 184 pp.

Schroeder, Walter A. *Missouri Water Atlas*. Rolla: Missouri Department of Natural Resources, Division of Geology and Land Survey, 1986. 97 pp.

Schuchard, Oliver, and Steve Kohler. *Two Ozark Rivers: The Current and the Jacks Fork*. Columbia: University of Missouri Press, 1984. 130 pp.

Schwartz, Charles W., and Elizabeth R. Schwartz. "Flying Mammals." In *The Wild Mammals of Missouri*, 51–98. Rev. ed. Columbia: University of Missouri Press and Missouri Department of Conservation, 1981.

Skinner, Brian J., and Stephen C. Porter. *The Dynamic Earth: An Introduction to Physical Geology*. New York: John Wiley & Sons, 1989. 541 pp.

Sloane, Bruce. *Cavers, Caves and Caving*. New Brunswick: Rutgers University Press, 1977. 409 pp.

Stitt, Robert, ed. *Cave Gating Handbook*. Huntsville: National Speleological Society, 1981. 60 pp.

————. "Wilderness Cave Management." In *National Cave Management Symposium Proceedings*, 53–56. Albuquerque: Speleobooks, 1976.

Thomson, Kenneth C. *Speleology: A Guide to the Study of Caves*. Springfield: Southwest Missouri State University, 1976. 120 pp.

Thomson, Kenneth C., and Ronald L. Martin. "An Introduction to Caving: A Guide for Beginners." *Missouri Speleology* 20:1–2 (1980): 43 pp.

Thomson, Kenneth C., and Robert L. Taylor. "An Introduction to Cave Mapping." *Missouri Speleology* 21:1–2 (1981): 123 pp.

Trost, Lucille Wood. *A Cycle of Seasons: The Little Brown Bat*. Reading: Young Scott Books, 1971. 48 pp.

Tuttle, Merlin. *America's Neighborhood Bats*. Austin: University of Texas Press, 1988. 96 pp.

U.S. Geological Survey and Missouri Division of Geological Survey and Water Resource.

Mineral and Water Resources of Missouri. Washington, D.C.: U.S. Government Printing Office, 1967. 399 pp.

Vandike, James E. "A Pleistocene Cat in a Missouri Cave." *National Cave Management Symposium Proceedings. Missouri Speleology* 25:1–4 (1985): 210–13.

Vineyard, Jerry D. "Cave Data Bases Revisited, 1984." *National Cave Management Symposium Proceedings. Missouri Speleology* 25:1–4 (1985): 117–32.

Vineyard, Jerry D., and Gerald L. Feder. *Springs of Missouri.* Rolla: Missouri Geological Survey and Water Resources, 1974. 267 pp.

Warren, Elizabeth. *I Can Read about Bats.* Mahwah, N.J.: Troll Associates, 1975. 48 pp.

Watson, Richard, and Roger Brucker. *Grand Kentucky Junction.* St. Louis: Cave Books, 1984. 96 pp.

Weaver, H. Dwight. "Caves: Missouri's Growing Natural Resource." *Missouri Resource Review* 7:2 (1990): 16–21.

———. "Early Gunpowder Making and Saltpeter Mining in Missouri Caves." *Journal of Spelean History* 4:1 (1971): 5–11.

———. *Great American Show Caves.* McMinnville, Tenn.: National Caves Association, 1982. 28 pp.

———. "Missouri's Underground Wilderness." *Missouri Resource Review* 4:1 (1987): 10–15.

Weaver, H. Dwight, and Paul A. Johnson. *Adventures at Mark Twain Cave.* Jefferson City: Discovery Enterprises, 1972. 64 pp.

———. *Meramec Caverns: Legendary Hideout of Jesse James.* Jefferson City: Discovery Enterprises, 1977. 126 pp.

———. *Missouri: The Cave State.* Jefferson City: Discovery Enterprises, 1980. 336 pp.

———. *Onondaga: The Mammoth Cave of Missouri.* Jefferson City: Discovery Enterprises, 1973. 94 pp.

Weinstock, Edward. *The Wilderness War.* New York: J. Messner, 1982. 191 pp.

White, William B. *Geomorphology and Hydrology of Karst Terrains.* New York: Oxford University Press, 1988. 464 pp.

Wiley, J. R. "Guide to the Amphibians of Missouri." *Missouri Speleology* 10:4 (1968): 132–72.

Wyckoff, Jerome. *Rock, Time, and Landforms.* New York: Harper & Row, 1966. 372 pp.

Yalden, D. W., and P. A. Morris. *The Lives of Bats.* New York: New York Times Book Co., 1975. 247 pp.

Zim, Herbert S. *Caves and Life.* New York: William Morrow and Co., 1978. 64 pp.

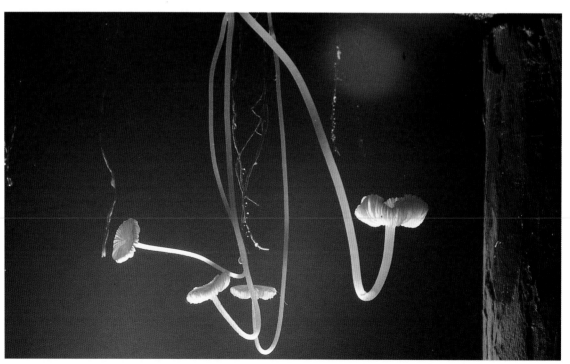

A delicate fungus grows from an old wood railing in a former commercial cave. Roy Gold

The Photographers

Emmet R. Anderson became interested in Ozark caves twenty-five years ago and recently combined his longtime love of photography with his caving activities. He is currently a graduate student in physics at the University of Arizona but is ambitious to return to the beautiful Ozarks.

Peter Chulick is intrigued by the fragile diversity and color of the underground environment. He began photographing caves twenty years ago, and the pursuit has led him into caves throughout the United States. Despite his active law practice in St. Louis, he still finds time to operate the Fendler-Chulick Funeral Home and to go caving.

Daniel Drees says that he is not an exceptionally talented photographer but his camera is always close at hand. He is a naturalist for the Missouri Department of Natural Resources at Meramec State Park, where caves are unusually plentiful. His profession grants him the good fortune of often being in just the right place at the right time to catch nature at its best.

Kevin Feltz works for the U.S. Fish and Wildlife Service. Photography was a natural extension of his love and appreciation of the earth and its history, be it natural or human. A photograph, he says, is like a painting because it reveals a great deal about the photographer's character. "I hope that my photography," he says, "reveals a

person who appreciates the great treasures this life has to offer."

James Glock began taking cave pictures nearly thirty years ago when he was first introduced to the beauty of the underground wilderness of the Ozarks. He is currently an electronics student at Linn Technical College and lives on Contrary Creek near the community of Welcome.

Robert Glock lives in Texas County in the very heart of the Missouri Ozarks. His employment with the U.S. Department of Agriculture Forest Service keeps him close to nature. Family camping and fishing trips during his youth led him to an appreciation of the Ozarks, a love that is reflected in his photography. His favorite leisure-time activities are canoeing, backpacking, and caving.

Roy Gold began caving in 1963 and eventually combined his interest in caves with photography. In the past he has explored Ozark caves in search of uncommon beauty to capture on film, but he is currently exploring and photographing a completely different kind of environment—the deserts and canyons of Colorado and Utah. He is a chemistry and math instructor at Colorado Northwestern Community College.

Art Hebrank is a geologist with the Missouri Department of Natural Resources, Division of Geology and Land Survey. For

The difficult task of surveying in a water passage requires extra time and preparation. Detailed cave maps provide information for research and may be used to determine the location of a cave relative to surface features. Robert L. Taylor

nearly thirty years he has pursued an active interest in caving, cave geology, and photography both as a hobby and as a profession. He currently conducts cave and karst geology workshops for schoolteachers as part of his environmental education work for the department.

James N. Huckins, a research environmental chemist for the U.S. Fish and Wildlife Service, learned the techniques of cave photography from masters of the art like Earl Neller, Jim Glock, Roy Gold, Pete Lindsey, and Carl Kunath. But he is also grateful for the assistance and insights that so many other cavers have given him, especially Cathy Huckins. He has served as a judge for the annual photography contest of the National Association for Conservation Information and says that his love of the Ozarks was originally inspired by his father's wonderful stories of early travels through the Ozarks and the natural beauty he encountered there.

John A. Lloyd began exploring Ozark caves without a camera in the early 1960s, but by 1970 his camera had become an essential piece of equipment for underground expeditions. The total darkness of the cave environment, he says, is a challenge to his creativity and gives him great pleasure. Other types of photography also appeal to him, including landscapes, wildlife, and old buildings.

Earl Neller is an archaeologist and for the past decade has been a cultural resource specialist for the Office of Hawaiian Affairs in Honolulu. He spends much of his time trying to protect and save endangered archaeological sites. His interest in Ozark caves began when he was a student at the University of Missouri, and he still takes his camera caving when he visits the mainland. He has contributed to the cave files maintained by the Missouri Speleological Survey and to Chouteau Grotto's journal, *Foresight.*

Terry Pitchford has focused much of his twenty-five years of speleological activity on the exploration of the vast cave systems of southeast Missouri. His interest in cave photography, he says, was a natural progression of his cave exploration, which stimulated a desire to capture on film some of the unique beauty he encountered beneath the Ozark Plateau. "Cave photography," he says, "is difficult and usually necessitates a team effort. I'm grateful to the other cavers who have assisted me."

James Ruth, a Columbia newspaper printer, developed his interest in photographing caves and related features of the Ozarks nearly thirty years ago when he was still in grade school. "Trips with my parents to visit caves and springs became as frequent as canoe trips on float streams," he says. "My interest in photography ensured that picture-taking would become an important part of the outings and my future."

Bruce Schuette lives at Troy, Missouri, and has been the park naturalist at Cuivre River State Park for eleven years. "During this time I have been building a collection of slides on all aspects of local natural history," he says. Several of his photographs have appeared in *Missouri Resource Review,* published by the Missouri Department of Natural Resources, and in brochures issued by the agency.

Scott Schulte is the superintendent at Rock Bridge Memorial State Park south of Columbia. He uses his camera to document the natural features of the two-thousand-acre park, which features the Devil's Icebox Cave, a historic natural rock bridge, and numerous sinkholes. He also enjoys photographing outdoor sports such as kayaking. His photographs have been used in slide shows produced by the Missouri Department of Natural Resources and have also appeared in a variety of publications.

Canyonlike passages such as this are typical of many Ozark caves. Robert L. Taylor

Dennis Taylor has been using photography to record the many scenic places he visits both above and below ground. He credits his improvement in photographic techniques to his association with the many fine photographers who are members of Chouteau Grotto. Dennis is currently exploring black-and-white photography with a medium-format camera.

Robert L. Taylor is pursuing his doctoral degree in philosophy at the University of Missouri–Columbia but still finds time to devote to his interests in photography, underground exploration, and cave surveying. He has been actively involved in all three activities since 1963. His photographs have appeared in the *NSS News*, *Missouri Speleology, High Country Times*, the *Official Guide to Marvel Cave*, and the *Geologic Wonders and Curiosities of Missouri*.

Richard Thom works in the natural history division of the Missouri Department of Conservation in Jefferson City. He has had a lifelong interest in photography, natural history, and caves. His writing and photographs frequently appear in the *Missouri Conservationist* magazine.

Merlin D. Tuttle is the founder and executive director of Bat Conservation International. He is a behavioral ecologist, wildlife photographer, and conservationist. He has published a book and more than forty scientific papers about bats and was the 1986 recipient of the Gerrit S. Miller, Jr., Award for outstanding service and contribution to the field of chiropteran biology. His photographs have been featured in many National Geographic publications and in major exhibits from Harvard University and the Smithsonian to the British Museum and the United Nations.

Unspoiled large columns and stalagmites give this scene a regal quality. James N. Huckins

Eugene Vale is a naturalist with the Missouri Department of Natural Resources and a graduate of St. Louis University. He became interested in caving and photography while in graduate school. After earning his A.B. and M.S.(R) in biology and a certificate in environmental studies, he found employment at an optico-electronics firm but spent his summer weekends working as a seasonal naturalist at Meramec State Park and Babler State Park. In 1985 he was appointed park naturalist at Onondaga Cave State Park.

James Vandike is a groundwater geologist with the Missouri Department of Natural Resources, Division of Geology and Land Survey. He became interested in caves and photography while in college and has spent much of the past thirteen years researching karst hydrology in the Missouri Ozarks. He is the author or coauthor of more than twenty publications, including articles for *Missouri Life* and the *Ozark Mountaineer.* His photographs have appeared in many newspapers, magazines, and textbooks.

Jerry D. Vineyard, deputy state geologist with the Missouri Department of Natural Resources, Division of Geology and Land Survey, began photographing caves in the early 1950s. His work has appeared in caving journals, books, and scientific papers. He was the principal photographer for the books *Springs of Missouri* and *Geologic Wonders and Curiosities of Missouri.*

Rickard L. Walk is a certified registered nurse anesthetist (CRNA) for Columbia Anesthesia Associates. He is a member of Chouteau Grotto, the Mid-Missouri Camera Club, and the Columbia Bicycle Club. He has been involved with photography since receiving his first camera from his grandmother. Over the past twelve years he has refined his photographic skills in the areas of mountaineering, rock climbing, and caving. His genuine love of the outdoors can be seen in his photography, which has appeared in calendars, the book *Colorful Missouri,* and the educational slide shows he provides for local schools and community groups.

*I*ndex

Numerals in bold type indicate illustrations

Abrasion: by rock particles, 25, 39
Acidity: of cave water, 55
Adaptations, by cave life: genetic, 13; to total darkness, 80
Aerated zone, 17, 21, 22, 25; definition of, 93
Aesthetic qualities: of caves, 1, 29; of speleogens, 35; of entrance zone, **36;** of waterfalls, 50; of speleothems, 50, 65, 72, 76
Age: of Ozark region, 4; of dolomites, 7, 9; of St. Francois Mountains, 8, 19; of Cambrian rock, 9; of Pre-Cambrian Era, 19; of solution process, 27; of solution features, 28; of air-filled caves, 28; of vertical shafts, 39; of sediments, 46; of prehistoric cat tracks, 86, **87**
Air flow in caves: mechanics of, 46
Albino cave life: cause of, 80. *See also* Cave life
Amblyopsis rosae. See Fish, cave: Ozark blind
American Indians: ancestors of, 8, 13, 86; use of caves, 13–15; use of red clay, 46
Ammonium nitrate: as a groundwater pollutant, 78
Amphipod, 77, 78
Animal remains: preserved in caves, 11, 13, 32, 86, **87**
Anthodite: crystals, 7, **88;** definition of, 93. *See also* Aragonite; Crystals
Aquifer, 21, 22; definition of, 93
Aragonite: crystals, 55, 60, **64;** spathite, 59; speleothems, **88;** definition of, 93. *See also* Anthodite; Crystals
Archaic Period, 13, 15. *See also* American Indians
Architecture, cave, 32, 35, 39
Arctotherium sp. *See* Bears: short-faced
Arkansas: cave resource protec-

tion act, 2; area of Ozarks in, 4; description of Ozarks in, 6; show caves, 6; recorded caves, 6, 17; mapped caves, 17
Arkansas River, 4
Artesian water pressure, 26; definition of, 93. *See also* Hydrostatic pressure
Atmosphere: of caves, 13; carbon dioxide in, 25

Bacon. *See* Drapery
Balconies. *See* Ledges
Banding: of chert, 19; of rhyolites, 19; of drapery, 65
Barometric pressure: and air flow, 46
Bats, 13, 80; protection of, 2; hibernation of, 47, 89; bones of, in calcite, **72;** gray (*Myotis grisescens*), 78, 84, **85;** echo location of, 84; big brown (*Eptesicus fuscus*), 84; eastern big-eared (*Plecotus rafinesquii*), 84; eastern pipistrelle (*Pipistrellus subflavus*), 84; Indiana (*Myotis sodalis*), 84; Keen's (*Myotis keenii*), 84; little brown (*Myotis lucifugus*), 84; Ozark big-eared (*Plecotus townsendii ingens*), 84; small-footed (*Myotis leibii*), 84; endangered species, 84, 85. *See also* Guano
Bears: beds of, 86; black (*Ursus americanus*), 86; short-faced (*Arctotherium* sp.), 86
Bedding plane, 21, 25, 39; definition of, 93
Bedrock: removal of, 9, 27, 28; thickness of, 19; composition of, 19; of Ozark Plateau, 20; joint systems, 21; water-bearing, 22; definition of, 50, 93
Beetles, 77, 80
Big Spring (Missouri), 25, **26;** size of, 11; flow of, 26. *See also* Dissolution: by groundwater; Watershed
Blanchard Springs Cavern (Ar-

kansas), **ii, iii, 6, 7, 30, 34, 40, 44, 54, 56, 70, 90**
Blind fish: cause of blindness, 80. *See also* Fish, cave: Ozark blind
Blue Spring (Missouri), **22**
Bluff Dwellers Cave (Missouri), 7
Boil: of springs, 26, **26**
Bones: preservation of, 65; bat, in calcite, **72;** in sediments, 86. *See also* Animal remains
Boston Mountains (Arkansas), **3;** description of, 6
Botryoid: definition of, 93
Breakdown, 6, 42, **43, 44;** definition of, 93
Bretz, J. Harlen: cave studies, 17; *Caves of Missouri*, 17
Bridal Cave (Missouri), 11
Bull Shoals Caverns (Arkansas), 6
Burlington limestone: crinoid fossil stems in, **20**

Caecidotera, **83.** *See also* Isopods
Calcite: helictites, **viii, 53;** crystals, 55, 56, **62;** precipitation of, 59, 65; "ice," 65; definition of, 93
Calcium carbonate, 19, 25, 55; definition of, 93
Calcium-magnesium carbonate, 19, 25; definition of, 93
Cambarus hubrichti. See Crayfish, cave: Salem
Cambarus setosus. See Crayfish, cave: bristly
Canopy: of flowstone, 65; definition of, 93
Canyon, **43;** definition of, 93. *See also* Channels; Chasms
Carbon dioxide, 25, 55, 59, 65, 62
Carbonic acid, 25; definition of, 93
Cat tracks, 86, **87.** *See also* Lion, American
Cave-fish. *See* Fish, cave